FLOWERS

THE COMPLETE BOOK OF FLORAL DESIGN

CHOOSING, CREATING, PRESENTING

BY **PAULA PRYKE**

PHOTOGRAPHS BY **KEVIN SUMMERS**

RIZZOLI

NEW YORK

Flowers: The Complete Book of Floral Design
Choosing, Creating, Presenting
Paula Pryke

For my mother and father who have been a constant
source of inspiration and love. My affection for flowers
began in the gardens that they tended and loved and I am
grateful for this passion and their support, which have
enriched my life.

First published in the United States of America in 2004 by
Rizzoli International Publications, Inc.
300 Park Avenue South
New York, NY 10010
www.rizzoliusa.com

Originally published in Great Britain in 2004 as
Classic Paula Pryke
by Mitchell Beazley, an imprint of
Octopus Publishing Group Ltd,
2–4 Heron Quays, London E14 4JP

Text © Paula Pryke 2004
Copyright Octopus Publishing Group Ltd 2004

ISBN-13: 978-0-8478-2643-8
Library of Congress Control Number: 2004105216

Third printing, 2007
2007 2008 2009 / 10 9 8 7 6 5 4 3

Senior Executive Editor **Anna Sanderson**
Art Director **Vivienne Brar**
Art Direction & Design **Robin Rout & Robin Rout Ltd**
Photographer **Kevin Summers**
Copy Editor **Anne McDowall**
Editor **Catherine Emslie**
Production Controller **Seyhan Esen**
Proofreader **Barbara Mellor**
Indexer **Sue Farr**

Front jacket An Isabel Stanley Ribbon vase filled with a
matching tied bunch of 'Milano' and 'Tressor 2000' gold roses,
'Prado' and burgundy carnations, blue anemones, germinis,
and gloriosa lilies.

Back jacket Clear Perspex vase filled with lines of roses, from
the top: 'Aqua', 'Milano', 'Coolwater', 'Black Bacarra', 'Ruby
Red', 'Aqua', 'Milano', 'Xtreme', 'Black Bacarra', 'Coolwater', and
'Milano' (see pages 164–5).

Half title A 'Malmaison' rose bouquet has been created by
using the petals of 'Coolwater', 'Milano', 'Grand Prix', 'Tressor
2000', 'Wow', and 'Rosita Vendelle'. Around the edge are the
vines of *Jasminum officinale* and varigated ivy (*Hedera helix*)
(see pages 38–9).

Title page White hellebores (*Helleborus niger*) woven into
horizontal stems of pussy willow (*Salix discolor*).

Set in Gill Sans

Printed and bound in China by
Toppan Printing Company Limited

Contents

6 | Introduction

8 | **Vision**
12 | Flower and foliage shapes
16 | Imitating flower shapes
18 | Nature's shapes and colours
20 | Imitating nature
22 | Unconventional designs
24 | Deconstructed designs
26 | Arrangement styles
28 | Containers

30 | **Classic**

106 | **Contemporary**

172 | **Techniques**

182 | **Flower Favourites**

234 | Index of botanical names

237 | General index

240 | Acknowledgments

Five calla lilies (Zantedeschia 'Mango') in an orange Macaroni glass vase.

Introduction: My life with flowers

In the mid-1980s I decided to pursue my dream of having a little flower shop. Working with beautiful flowers and spending most of the day creating attractive gifts that will please their recipients is, understandably, a popular aspiration, and a career in floristry is one that many people from diverse backgrounds and careers hanker after.

For me it was the start of a passion that has taken many interesting directions over the last two decades, and it has been a fascinating journey. I had no idea when I began my flower business in 1988 that this was to be the start of a whole new approach to commercial flower design and amateur flower arranging and that my work would become influential around the world.

My first book, which was published in 1993 – just five years after I took the plunge to change career from history teacher to florist – has been translated into many languages and has been sold to flower enthusiasts all over the world.

None of this would have been possible without the love and devotion of my husband Peter, who has shared me with this passion.

Paula Pryke

This arrangement has been created by attaching leeks (*Allium ampeloprasum*) to a container with raffia and then adding a late summer mixture of sunflowers (*Helianthus annus*), zinnias, dill (*Anethum graveolens*), 'Black Magic' roses, *Leucadendron* 'Safari Sunset', and tropical gingers (*Zingiber zerumbet*).

Vision

Gerbera 'Doctor Who'

Floral vision

One of the questions I am most frequently asked is "Where do you get your ideas from?" Inspiration comes from a huge range of external sources, but as floral design is such an ephemeral art form, I am sure that working under pressure to so many deadlines has been the most focusing factor in my creative process! Then, of course, there are the clients who can't find anything they like in my portfolio and who want me to create a new design that takes into consideration their particular preferences, likes, and dislikes. In my business, I have been in the fortunate position of often working alongside other creative people – architects, designers, photographers, sculptors, artists, garden designers – and innovative ideas will often emerge from this experience, which inspires me to see floral design from new directions. Themed parties, product launches, openings, and galas all provide their own briefs and themes, and new ideas will develop as I begin to work.

But for me, nature itself is the most important creative force in my work. Inspiration may come from observing an individual flower or leaf pattern, a new variety, or the much wider picture of an interesting landscape. A rainbow-coloured field of ranunculus in Carlsbad, California; a lavender farm in Norfolk; the twisted and gnarled vines growing among the mustard in Sonoma Valley; the heathery and rocky slopes of the Highlands of Scotland; the sunset over a field of wheat – all have influenced both my life and my art.

This living topiary tree was created by arranging a group of 'Telstar' amaryllis (Hippeastrum) with their heads at the same height, binding them just below the flower heads. Their stems are impaled on a 3in (8cm) pin holder, which is concealed with pebbles.

Panicle (*Oncidium*) When masses of small blossoms are found on many branching stems, the form is known as a panicle. Oncidium orchids are a good example, as too is the bushy blossom of lilac.

Flower and foliage shapes

There is an enormous diversity of shapes and patterns in the plant world and some study and understanding of them is essential if you want to create striking flower arrangements. Most floral designs will feature a number of different attractive forms displayed together. My simple philosophy on flower arranging is that you should be able to take a group of flowers and foliages that are individually appealing and create a composition that enhances their beauty. A harmonious combination of plant material will be more pleasing to the eye than a mismatch of flowers and foliages that have been chosen hastily or carelessly.

When you first begin to select flower combinations you will inevitably be drawn to your favourite flowers, but if they do not enhance one another in your intended design, they will not make an attractive display. For example, five of my favourite flowers are lily-of-the-valley (*Convallaria*), sweet peas (*Lathyrus odoratus*), grape hyacinths (*Muscari*), roses, and forget-me-nots (*Myosotis*). Although all five will complement each other beautifully in a hand-tied posy, the combination would look fussy in a small table arrangement, as many of the shapes are too weak and small. And of course, they would be completely ineffectual in a large design.

The successful unity of three factors underlines all good floral composition: colour, form, and function. The more you study and truly understand each individual flower with these aspects of it in mind, the better equipped you will be to produce designs that combine them in harmonious and appealing ways. You will find, too, that your creativity is unleashed.

The floral designer need be concerned with only a few of the basic characteristics of plants. Because all flowers exist to reproduce the plants they adorn, all conform to the same basic structure. In the centre of the flower are the female reproduction organs, known collectively as the pistil, and home to the style, stigma (which receives pollen), and the ovary. The male reproductive organs are the stamens, which include the filament – the stalk of the anther (which produces pollen). These are nestled on the perianth, which is the union of the base or calyx and the sepals, from which corolla or petals emerge. The relationship between the stem and the number of flowers is called the inflorescence. There are many different types of inflorescence, and here we have identified some of the most common and important for floral design.

Branch (*Eustoma*) Lisianthus has an erect branching stem which is irregular and asymmetrical in its form. The ends of the stems are arched, which makes this flower a very useful addition to small and medium arrangements and hand-ties, where its branching stems give movement to the design.

Spike (*Moluccella laevis*) The spiked bells of Ireland adds elegance and a linear shape to vases and large designs. For colour, use larkspur (*Consolida*), monkshood (*Aconitum*), and delphiniums, all of which have similarly elongated clusters of flowers.

Corymb (*Sedum*) The round shape of the sedum is formed by a cluster of blossoms branching from a straight erect stem. Corymb-shaped flowers are useful as fillers and also create a lovely textural effect in floral designs. They are also perfect for massed arrangements where the heads are used compactly.

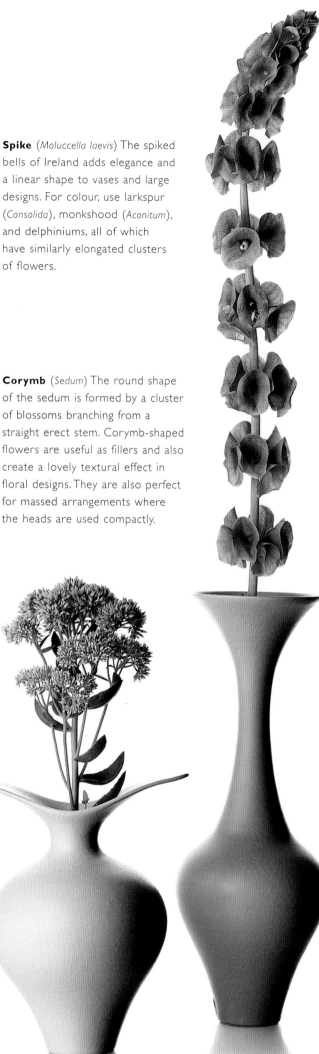

Umbel (*Anethum graveolens*) One of my favourite flower shapes is the umbel, where spikes of inflorescence come from one central stem. Many wild flowers and herbs have this shape, including dill (shown here), cow parsley, and angelica.

Star (*Iris*) Star-shaped flowers such as iris and lilies are excellent to use on their own because they are visually very strong. They also make a great shape in mixed arrangements, where their distinct form means they will often be used as dominant flowers.

Composite (*Gerbera*) A round shape like that of a daisy is known as a composite. Flowers with a composite shape vary enormously in size, from tiny dandelions to huge sunflowers. Although their scale differs, however, their use does not: these perfectly shaped flowers are invariably focal points.

Bell (*Zantedeschia*) Bell-shaped flowers or coneflowers, such as calla lilies, will always be very strong and dominant in a design. There are many distinct shapes within this category, certainly too many to classify them all individually here.

Rosette (*Cynara*) Another textural form I am fond of is the rosette, where a number of leaves appear to form a flower shape. Brassicas, artichokes, and many succulents have a rosette shape.

Umbel   Star   Composite   Bell   Rosette   Simple

Simple (*Papaver*) Simple-shaped flowers, such as the poppy, violet (*Viola*), and wood lily (*Trillium*), have fewer petals – normally four or five, occasionally three or six. Most simple flowers are radially symmetrical and the individual flowers tend to stand out separately. Passionflowers (*Passiflora*), pansies (*Viola wittrockiana*) and hellebores (*Helleborus*) are also examples of this shape.

Irregular (*Paphiopedilum*) There are many different flowers that have an irregular or odd shape, but the orchid family provides some good examples. Flowers like this are usually dominant and are often used individually. They create good focal points and interesting textures.

Globular (*Echinops*) Spherical flowers are known as globular and can be very simple. Round balls are dominant: they may be textural, such as the craspedia and the globe thistle (*Echinops*), or huge and rather architectural, like the giant onion flowers (*Allium*).

Unusual (*Anthurium*) Another irregular and unusual shape is the spadix of anthuriums, which creates a very strong visual statement and is therefore used as a focal flower.

Raceme (*Delphinium*) When a number of flowers are found on the stem, this is called a raceme. The pointed astilbe is another good example and is useful for filling arrangements.

Irregular   *Globular*   *Unusual*   *Raceme*

Imitating flower shapes

The organic world has been a source of inspiration to artists throughout history. The shapes present in nature have been used as models by potters, glassblowers, sculptors, and artisans working in all kinds of media. The natural world has also been very influential in architecture, where vegetative forms have found their way into details and styles from the richly adorned Corinthian columns of the Parthenon and the dome-shape structure of mosques to the tendrils and turrets in Gothic architecture.

Floral designers will often imitate the shapes of individual flowers or foliage in larger arrangements. The study of different flower heads can teach you a lot about balance and proportion in floral design. The rosette form found in succulents and members of the brassica family is a very easy design to imitate using other flowers, leaves, and petals. A tightly packed bouquet of red anthuriums will give the same effect. The reconstructed rose bouquet shown on the half title page of this book exaggerates the petal effect found in composite flower shapes.

The globular or spherical shape is found throughout the natural world, in flower heads, berries, and fruits, and is certainly one of the easiest to imitate. For example, the globe thistle shape consists of a tight, spiky receptacle with a radial of purple tubular petals, and this shape can be re-created using a globe-shaped case and tubular flowers mixed with spiky witch hazel.

Examining the form of the wild and unruly plants found in nature will help you understand more about asymmetrical design. The wild shape found in branches of catkins inspired me to create a trailing asymmetrical design of orchids, for example.

A more open flower shape, such as that of aquilegias, can be a great inspiration for a symmetrical front-facing arrangement. The design is essentially triangular in shape, but the plant material will need to radiate from the centre and be in perfect balance. More open plant forms encourage flower designers to use shapes that are more contrived, and for this reason this is my least favourite form.

Formal topiary arrangement *left*
To create this lollipop tree, cement a birch trunk (approximately 18in/45cm long and 1¾in/4.5cm thick) into a plastic pot that will fit snugly into the bottom of an urn. Place two blocks of soaked florist's foam around the base of the stem and tape the foam ball on the top. Add chrysanthemums to the ball and the base of the stem, I used forty stems of *Chrysanthemum* (Indicum Gr.) 'Fred Shoesmith', then wind a length of clematis vine around the stem.

The hairy, twisted stems of these burnt-orange
Iceland poppies (Papaver nudicaule) – loosely
arranged in a beautiful golden glass vase by
Catherine Hough – are as interesting as the
flowers themselves and deserve to be admired.

Floral design often imitates shapes from nature, and the trailing proportions of this giant fly-catcher pitcher plant (Nepenthes maxima) are very inspirational. Arrangements in which the proportions are directed downward is this way are very popular in European floral design, where plant material may be wired together to create an elegant cascade. Sometimes berries or seed heads are wired onto grasses or threaded to imitate the formation of this pitcher plant.

Submerged roses in a bulb vase *right*

Three rose heads (*Rosa* 'Illusion') have been wired and weighted underwater with a stone, submerged beneath the amaryllis bulb (*Hippeastrum* 'Apple Blossom'). Submerged flowers or arrangements in water have become fashionable in recent years. Flower food mixed into the water helps to keep the water clear.

Topiary with nerines *far right*

Ten nerines (*Nerine bowdenii* 'Corusca Major') have been tied together just below their heads to create a living topiary, with the stems cut to the desired length. Five roses (*Rosa* 'Ruby Red'), their stems cut short, have been placed around the base of the nerine stems so that their flower heads sit in the wide rim of this elegant black vase, designed by Vivienne Foley.

Nature's shapes and colours

There is an enormous amount that you can learn from studying not only the shapes of individual flowers, but also the fundamentals of good colour design that are to be found within the natural world. Although there are some basic rules of colour theory that you can learn, these are often detached from their context in nature. In the natural world, no colour is ever seen in isolation, and this is true even in the case of individual flowers. For example, a red gerbera may have a yellow or black eye and a green stem, while the creamy powder of the catkin is found on a chocolate-brown stem. Nature is complex, and every flower colour interacts with others, making it more than a little difficult to give absolute rules on colour theory.

The "personality" of a flower derives from both its shape and its colour. The shades and tints found even within a single flower – cool, warm, deep, intense – are often quite diverse. The translucency or opacity of each petal or leaf will also influence how you perceive the flower and how you may use it. These natural nuances defy any artificial man-made rules on design and colour, and for me this is one of the most enjoyable aspects of working with flowers.

Look to individual flowers for lessons on colour harmonies and for good shapes. Red and green are often represented by berries or hips, or pure flower colour, and the two colours are very pleasing together: the intense red with the more restful green is a perfect combination of complementary colours that complies with conventional colour theory. Yellow and blue are found among the pansies, violets, and irises, and although these colours contrast with one another, they also create a harmony. Orange and purple is not a combination for the faint-hearted, but it can be seen in bird of paradise flowers (*Strelitzia*) and in 'Princess Irene' tulips. The acid-pink gloriosa with its limey yellow edge offers a hint of another great, though daring, colour combination, while the burgundy nose of the cymbidium orchid mixes well with many other colours, from pale pink to bright yellow and vivid green.

You can also learn much from the individual shape and habit of a flower. Amaryllis (*Hippeastrum*) and nerines are excellent examples: both are bulb flowers that have long elegant stems and large heads. The amaryllis usually has four flowers at the top of its wide hollow stem, while the nerine is a multi-flowered umbel. By placing several of them together and creating a living topiary, you are imitating their form in nature to create a very simple, elegant design.

Simple anemone hand-tie *above*
This hand-tied arrangement of 'Mona Lisa White' anemones has been trimmed
to sit in a cube glass vase as a "standing bouquet" tree. Skeletonized leaves
have been attached to the sides of the vase using spray glue.

Imitating nature

*Observing and enjoying nature has probably given
me more personal inspiration for new floral designs
than any other single source. I believe that a love of
nature translates directly into how successful a
design is and how accomplished a florist you can
become. There are many competent florists who do
not have enough empathy with their plant material
to create really great floral designs. They are able
to re-create formulaic flower arrangements, but are
not inspired enough by the flowers and plants
themselves to be truly innovative. An arrangement
has that extra magical quality – admittedly hard to
define – when the florist has made an emotional
statement after intimately observing his or her
plant material.*

Nature offers huge inspiration, as well as indicating how to handle
plant material. Learning about the structure of plants can help you
to create good shapes, and by studying nature you gain valuable
insights into which flowers and plants work well together. Adopting a
holistic approach to floral design will, I believe, enable you to make
far more of your flowers, and ultimately will help you to become a
far better floral designer. By observing a single straight stem with a
large head – an amaryllis (*Hippeastrum*), agapanthus, or a nerine – or
a perfectly clipped privet (*Ligustrum*) or box topiary tree, you will
gain insight into harmonious and classic shapes. Look at the shapes
made by larger groups, too: the outline of a group of hornbeams
(*Carpinus*) on a hill or the bare leafless structure of a some horse-
chestnut trees (*Aesculus*) in autumn will help you gain a sense of
what might work well in floral design.

The tied topiary arrangement of sunflowers (right) is an
example of a design that is simple –and fairly straightforward to
create – and yet quite grand. A "living topiary" design like this can be
created with most straight-stemmed flowers and particularly suits
round-headed flowers – anemones, daisies, and gerberas, for
example – and multi-petalled round shapes, such as ranunculus,
dianthus, and roses. Star-shaped flowers with multiple heads, such as
nerines, agapanthus, and narcissus, with their slender and elegant
stems and larger heads, also work well in this type of design.

Living topiary sunflower tree *left*

Cover a 12in (30cm) tall glass vase with doubled-sided tape, then, using a low-heat glue gun, attach snake grass (*Equisetum*) vertically around the side. (Double-sided tape alone is insufficient to hold the grass in place but makes it easier to remove the glue from the vase.) Tie thirty sunflowers with 40in (1m) stems just below their heads to create a round ball. Attach a 3in (8cm) pin-holder inside the vase, then fix the sunflower stems to its uprights. Pack sphagnum moss round the stems and top up the vase with water. Finally, add a few sunflower leaves around the top of the vase.

Multicoloured ranunculus in leafed glass *above*

Place double-sided tape around the outside of a tall glass tumbler and arrange rhododendron leaves to cover it (I have placed some vertically and wrapped others around the base). Create a dome of mixed coloured ranunculus by hand-tying them into a spiral posy – you will need about fifty stems. Cut the stems to fit into the glass to create a tree-like design.

Unconventional designs

Traditionally, flower arrangements have had only one focal point – or centre of growth, as it is known in European floristry. More recently, however, attractive floral designs have evolved that have two or more points of interest and several layers to them. Such arrangements are often created without any reference to the conventional rules of design and do not fit under any traditional style headings. The florist is free to experiment, to express his or her fantasies with flowers, and to disregard all the rules. But it is worth remembering that it takes experience as well as understanding – of the plant material and of the basic principles of design – to ensure that experimental floral arrangements of this kind are still pleasing to the eye.

Although the rules governing ikebana were established in Japan more than a thousand years ago, only since the 1930s has flower arranging been seen as a serious craft or art form in the West. One of the first floral design experts was Constance Spry, who started her London school in 1935 and opened another, in New York, in 1937. There had been a few before her who had written about floral design, however, including Josiah Condor, who studied ikebana in Japan more than a hundred years ago, and Gertrude Jekyll, who wrote *Floral Decoration in the House* in 1907 and was the first to use wire mesh as a mechanic in floral arrangements. Gradually, amateur flower arranging groups and societies of floristry for professionals started to emerge, and the principles and "rules" of flower arranging became firmly established.

Over the last twenty years or so there has been an enormous growth in the creative side of the industry, and a huge interest in unconventional and contemporary arrangements. In some ways, such designs are easier to create, but, as with all fashions, styles in floral design come and go. And so the truly accomplished floral designer needs to be able to work in all genres and to understand the rules in order to be able to break the mould and produce truly creative work with integrity.

Heliconia and vine *left*
Heliconias are excellent flowers to submerge because their big fleshy flowers do not decompose or contaminate the water. This striking arrangement uses four heliconias (*Heliconia stricta* 'Firebird'), one of which is submerged upside down in the vase. A length of honeysuckle vine (*Lonicera periclymenum* 'Serotina') is loosely wrapped around the stems.

Strelitzia ring *right*
The base of this unconventional design is the centre of its growth and the main focal area, but the eye is also drawn up to the flower heads of the architectural birds of paradise (*Strelitzia*). See pages 152–3 for instructions on how to make a similar arrangement.

Deconstructed designs

Rather than create a composition of flowers from different genera, a recent fashion in floral design has been to use just one type of flower. In its purest form, such a design may use a single colour of one variety (such as the arrangement of vanda orchids shown on the right). Or it may consist of groups of different colours of one flower (as with the collection of gerberas shown below). Alternatively, a number of varieties of the same colour could be displayed in their own containers and enjoyed together as a centrepiece.

Composite arrangements such as these are currently very fashionable for hotel foyers and in other corporate work, where opulent but simple displays are often assembled together almost in imitation of the banks of flowers in a flower shop.

In its most extreme form, a deconstructed floral design may take a single part of a flower and reconstruct it into another form, as with the kebab of petals shown on the left, or the rose structure on pages 38–9, where roses have been taken apart and their petals used to create a much larger-headed "rose". The deconstruction movement, which started in Europe, is now being imitated in floral designs all over the world. Such designs are often influenced by the way flowers are used in the Far East, where masses of flower heads of one genus may be used to create leis or garlands.

Above A kebab of mixed rose petals skewered on a bamboo cane. This kind of floral design imitates the use of flowers and petals in Asian cultures, where petals or whole flower heads are often threaded together to create garlands and tokens of welcome.

Right Seven coloured bullet glasses are assembled together to display a collection of gerbera daisies – three stems in each glass. However simple an arrangement, its effect is magnified when several identical vases are grouped in this way.

Far right Pink vanda orchids are displayed in elegant zinc bottles. The duplication of a simple idea creates a new arrangement. In my opinion, repetition works best with simple designs such as domes of roses, topiary trees of one flower, or single stems in vases, as shown here.

Asymmetrical arrangement *above*
Start with the taller flowers, arranging stems of pink ginger (*Alpinia purpurata*) so that they all face the same way. Add banksia (*Banksia collina*) on the right and leucospermums (*Leucospermum cordifolium* 'Red Sunset') on the left. Next, position the king proteas (*Protea cynaroides*) and *Protea graniceps* in the centre, with three waratahs (*Telopea speciosissima*) to the front. Place kentia palm leaves at opposite sides of the vase to give balance and movement. Finally, soften the edges and highlight the asymmetry with a bunch of coral fern (*Gleichenia polypodiodes*) on the right-hand side.

Arrangement styles

There are some classic flower arrangement shapes that I use a lot throughout my work and that you will need to master if you are to be a successful flower arranger. Once you are proficient at creating classic styles and shapes, you are ready to develop and hone your own style. The free style that you will be able to adopt will follow the same principles of rhythm, balance, harmony, scale, and proportion. A great use of colour and texture and a feeling of movement will also enhance a design. In European floristry this free style approach is known as decorative floristry.

Symmetrical Arrangements that are perfectly balanced on either side and generally front facing are usually quite formal. Symmetrical designs can be rigid and, in my opinion, uninteresting.
Asymmetrical You will notice that most of my work is lacking in symmetry, like the design shown on the left, for example. Asymmetrical shapes are looser, much more versatile, and can be used in large or small arrangements.
Round Another very important and popular design shape is the round or circular one. These designs need to be perfect when seen from all angles and are often used for table centrepieces, as well as in other decorative arrangements.
Line As the name suggests, this type of arrangement is usually quite minimal and may consist of a staggered line of one or two flowers and some foliage. Line arrangements take their inspiration from oriental design and the ikebana school of flower arranging. I find that this kind of design is useful for contract work or for commissions where the budget is limited.
Topiary Massed arrangements – usually in a round or cone shape – are particularly useful for special occasions and festive decorations. The topiary arrangement on the right is very small and suitable for a table centrepiece, but topiary forms can be equally useful devices for creating vast floral displays. Indeed, this kind of structure can be the safest way to create large columns of flowers – the largest topiary cone arrangement I have ever made stood nearly 20ft (6m) tall!
Natural or vegetative The design shown on the far right uses seasonal flowers in a form that mirrors their natural habitat. The aim of a vegetative arrangement is generally to imitate the way in which you would expect to see the plants in the wild, making them look almost as if they were still growing.
Parallel This style of arrangement developed in the 1980s, principally in the Netherlands. Parallel designs use groups of stems that stand vertically. They can be massed or minimal, but most often use plant material in a natural way.

Multicoloured topiary arrangement *left*

Pack damp sphagnum moss into the centre of a wire topiary cone, then wire this securely into an old terracotta pot. This arrangement uses kumquats, lychees, pattypans, physalis, mauve hydrangea heads (*Hydrangea macrophylla*), branches of bright green bupleurum (*Bupleurum griffithii*), brightly coloured zinnias, and everlasting flowers (*Helichrysum bracteatum*). Wire each flower head and piece of fruit individually, then push the wire mounts into the cone to create a patchwork of colour. Mist the finished topiary with water and attach a matching silk bow around the top of the pot.

Spring vegetative bark box *above*

This vegetative arrangement uses seasonal flowers that you would find together in the wild. To create the impression that they are growing, the foam needs to be flush with the edge of the bark box and covered with moss. Begin by adding tall yellow irises – *Iris* (Hollandse Iris Gr.) 'Apollo', double daffodils (*Narcissus* 'Golden Ducat'), and achillea (*Achillea millefolium* 'Inca Gold'), then place sprigs of bear grass (*Xerophyllum tenax*) throughout to give movement. Place widow iris (*Hermodactylus tuberosa*) along the box in different directions. Finally add the miniature daffodils (*Narcissus* 'Charity May') and lachenalia (*Lachenalia* 'Quadricolour') at the front of the box. Use a few of the smaller sprigs of achillea to fill any gaps.

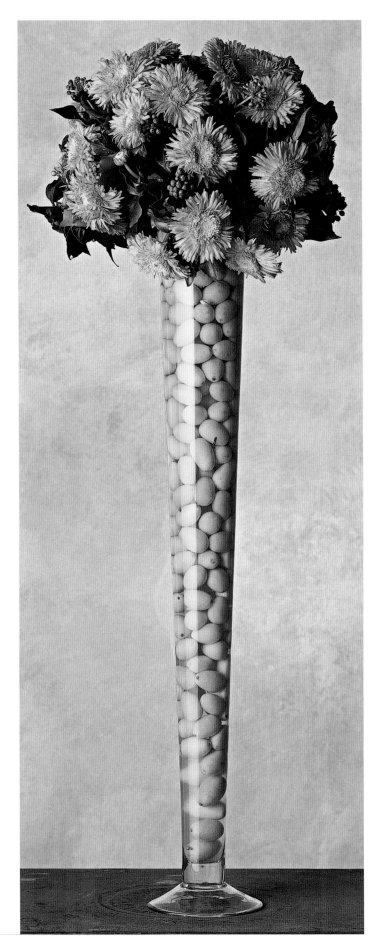

Containers

One of the trademarks of my floral style has been the incorporation of the container into the design. Glassware has been a staple of many of my arrangements. Initially I used lots of pieces of glassware that had not originally been intended for flower arrangements, but innovative floral design has become more and more popular, and much glassware is now designed specifically with the floral market in mind.

Twenty years ago I would often conceal pots by attaching plant material – often with double-sided tape, sometimes using a glue gun – around the outside of the container. This was, and is, a great way to disguise a cheap or ugly container.

Later on, the trend developed for more minimal and sleeker arrangements. Glassware is obviously ideal for creating such a look and I began to use flowers and other plant material inside the vases too. This new style suits the current fashions for interiors and – like good ikebana arrangements – it makes the most of one flower type, often focusing attention on a single bloom. It is therefore a modern twist on a very old idea.

Throughout my work I have often used fruit and vegetables to complement flowers. However, as both give off the same ageing hormone, ethylene, it is advisable to use these other natural resources only when the arrangement is for a special occasion when the longevity of the design is not crucial. I like using these other natural ingredients because of their textures and colours and because they often add a freshness and that extra "wow" factor to decorations for a party or celebration.

Finding new containers and adapting old ones continues to be an inspiring force and integral to my floral design.

Kumquat arrangement *left*
Arrange thirty stems of marigolds (*Calendula officinalis*) with a few stems of ivy berries (*Hedera helix*) in a hand-tied bunch (see page 177). Add some more stems of ivy berries around the edge to protect the flowers and to allow the ivy to trail over the sides of the vase. Tie the bunch and trim the stems short. Fill a 40in (1m) long flared glass vase with kumquats – you will need about two boxes – then place the hand-tie in the top and add water.

Ten stems of gloriosa (Gloriosa rothschildiana) have been twisted inside a globe fishbowl. Make sure that the ends of the stems are in the base of the vase so that they are submerged in the water.

Classic

Crown of snowdrops

Snowdrops have a special significance as the harbingers of spring: the advent of these tiny brave flowers marks the start of the wonderful cycle of regrowth and the awakening of the plant world after the long dormant months of winter. Their fragile appearance belies an exceptional hardiness, as they are the first flowers to pierce through the frozen topsoil.

White, for me, is symbolic of the new year, and I am particularly drawn to it after the decorative excesses of the Christmas season. Interestingly, although white flowers can be found throughout the world, they predominate in the colder northern climates. This was one of the first things that the Romans noticed about Britain and may well account for their bestowing the name of "Albion" on England (though historians are divided as to whether this name came from the white cliffs of Dover — the first sight that would have greeted the invaders — or the wild white roses that covered most of the country then).

White flowers always look elegant: indeed, they are the flower world's equivalent of the little black dress — they are always in fashion and suit any interior.

Low arrangements of concentric circles of flowers like this were very popular in the Victorian period.

Fill an antique urn with soaked florist's foam so that it is a least an inch higher than the edge of the container. Begin by edging the urn with glossy green ivy leaves to hide the foam and create a trail over the edge of the container. Next place the ranunculus in a round circle in the middle of the urn, starting with a central flower and working outward in circles. After about three rows you will be ready to add a circle of the lovely green balls of the guelder roses.

The snowdrops, which form the outer ring, are fragile to place in the foam, so you will need to wire them. Bunch about ten together, trim them, and add a double leg mount. To do this, take a medium-gauge stub wire and bend it into a hairpin shape, then wind one leg over the other three times to create a two-pronged mount. Use this wire mount to anchor the ends of the stems into the foam.

Ingredients

Flowers & foliage
Ivy berries (*Hedera helix*)
Ranunculus (*Ranunculus* 'Ranobelle Inra White')
Guelder rose (*Viburnum opulus*)
Snowdrops (*Galanthus nivalis* 'Flore Pleno')

Other materials
Antique urn
Florist's foam
Medium-gauge stub wires

Lollipop topiary

The topiary arrangement is another staple floral design that comes in and goes out of fashion with regularity, but it is popular for weddings and, of course, for the festive season. At its simplest, a topiary form can be created by attaching a block of foam to a branch that has been secured into a heavy pot. Most of my topiary designs are specially made by soldering an iron box onto a birch or bamboo pole and then cementing it into an appropriate base to give it stability.

Ingredients

Flowers & foliage
Camellia (*Camellia japonica*)
Bunch of fountain grass
(*Panicum vergatum* 'Fountain')
Hydrangea (*Hydrangea macrophylla* 'Green Shadow')
Sedum (*Sedum spectabile*)
10 chrysanthemum
(*Chrysanthemum* [Indicum Gr.]
'Delistar')
Bunch of pink snowberries
(*Symphoricarpos* 'Pink Pearl')
12 green roses (*Rosa* 'Eden')

Other materials
Topiary frame
Florist's foam

1 A purpose-built box frame has here been designed specifically to hold half a block of soaked florist's foam. The wire box is made using a soldering iron, and this one has then been cemented into a terracotta pot. This rustic autumn topiary has been designed to sit on a table for an birthday party. When the mechanics are complete – and this is very important for topiary as it needs to be stable and not top heavy – you can begin to work on the shape of the design.

Take small pieces of foliage of the same length and arrange them all around the frame to create the ball of the topiary. Keep moving the frame around as you are working so that you can see it from all angles and ensure that it is rounded. Strong dense foliage such as camellia is ideal for this: ruscus, salal, and fruiting ivy would all be good substitutes. Choose at least three different types of foliage to create interest.

2 Next add the soft and spiky fountain grass that gives the arrangement movement, and the green hydrangea heads and sedum, which are very dense and textural. When the foam is almost covered, you can begin to place the flowers. I have chosen a number of different-shaped flowers for this. The round roses are probably the most commonly used for this kind of arrangement, and I have contrasted these with spiky chrysanthemums and soft berries. Start with chrysanthemum blooms around the ball at different heights and not too close to one another. Then add little sprays of the pink snowberries and finally the green spray roses, placing them all around the ball in the gaps. Make sure that you are still keeping a good round shape.

Topiary arrangements can be made ahead of an event: position the foliage two or three days beforehand, leaving the flowers to be added the day before.

Symphoricarpos 'Red Pearl'

White vase arrangement

Cool and serene, white is soothing to look at and its neutrality complements every other colour. This makes it the most versatile shade in the florist's palette, offering enormous possibilities for all sorts of arrangements. Strictly speaking, white is not a colour: the colour we perceive as white is really a reflection of light. Traditionally, white is associated with purity and innocence, and in many cultures white flowers are used for celebratory and commemorative occasions, such as weddings, christenings, and other spiritual events. A high proportion of white flowers are scented, which is another reason for their popularity. Brides often choose white flowers such as jasmine, lily-of-the-valley, stephanotis, tuberosa, gardenia, and freesia for their bridal bouquets – as much for their scent as for the colour. White is also chosen more than any other colour for remembrance or sympathy flowers, and so for some white flowers are synonymous with sad occasions. Some white flowers are also very stylish – lilies work particularly well in vase arrangements.

To create a simple and elegant massed vase arrangement like this, you need to choose a number of different shapes. Start by arranging the foliage so that you have a good structure in which to place the first flowers. The dark ruscus has a good trail and the eucalyptus is busy, and supportive to the flowers. The tall spikes of white delphiniums and campanula make an excellent outline and so define the size of the arrangement, drawing your eyes toward its extremities. The star-shaped lilies create impact and add scent, and the round shape of the open roses and peonies makes them good focal flowers. Bouvardia has been added to catch the light and trachelium to fill any holes and gaps.

Following the classic guidelines for proportion, this traditional vase arrangement is one and half times the height of its container.

Ingredients

Flowers & foliage
Ruscus (*Danäe racemosa*)
Eucalyptus
(*Eucalyptus polyanthemos*)
Delphinium
(*Delphinium elatum* 'Ned')
Campanula
(*Campanula cochleariifolia*)
Lilies (*Lilium* 'Casablanca')
Roses (*Rosa* 'Bianca')
Peonies (*Paeonia* 'Gardenia')
Bouvardia (*Bouvardia* 'Caroline')
Trachelium (*Trachelium* 'Helios')

Deconstructed rose

The idea of taking one flower, dissecting it, and creating a new design has been popular for well over half a century. Originally the technique was used to create larger wired flower heads to wear as buttonholes. Such designs traditionally used spray carnations, or occasionally roses before such large hybrids were available. In earlier years, each flower petal had to be individually wired; these days we can re-create such designs much more speedily with the use of florist's adhesive.

Ingredients

Flowers & foliage
Bunch of galax leaves
(*Galax aphylla*)
20 roses (*Rosa* 'Vendelle')
1 bead vine plant
(*Crassula rupestris*)

Other materials
Circle of stiff cardboard
Florist's adhesive
A few 0.9mm florist's wires
Bundle of silver 0.22mm wires
Vine bouquet holder

1 Cut a circle of cardboard 3in (8cm) in diameter as the backing for this posy. Next glue some galax leaves to the front and back of the cardboard circle. Galax laves are available all year round and are very long lasting, but you could also use salal, ivy, or oak leaves. Any liquid glue suitable for sticking cardboard will work fine. I do not recommend a glue gun for this, as it may scorch the leaves.

2 Pick the best rose from the bunch – it should have a really perfect centre. Make a hairpin from 0.9mm wire and push both ends through the rose's calyx, bringing the two lengths of wire together. Using the points of your floristry scissors, make a hole in the centre of the leaf-covered circle. Now pinch out the petal centre of another rose and, using small hairpins made from 0.22mm wires, attach these petals to the side of the central rose.

3 Continue pinning petals around the central rose until it resembles a giant cabbage rose and you have almost completely covered the leafed backing card. Then place the covered disk onto the vine bouquet holder (commonly used in European floristry these are now quite widely available). Finally (right), attach bead plant vines around the edge of the frame, using silver wires to secure them in place, so the roses are framed by the green beads.

Rosa 'Vendelle'

Sheaf of grasses

The hand-tied bouquet with stems spiralled to create an arrangement that can stand on its own is a very old design that started life as a functional form rather than as a decorative one. It follows the same natural principles as farmers used for years to stack their crops into sheaves after the summer harvest. This simple motif can be found in art going back centuries, and is shown well in this arrangement of grasses, reeds, and seed heads standing on their own stems. The principle of a hand-tied bouquet is that the stems should all be spiralled in the same direction. If the stems cross the design will look unbalanced, and this will be particularly noticeable once all the stems are tied together. The techniques for hand-tied bouquets are very simple (see Techniques, page 177), but they need repeated practice if you are to achieve successful results. The key to creating a good bunch is to keep the binding point very clean and to continue to twist the stems in your hands so that you are working equally on all sides of the arrangement. While you are learning it is a good idea to practise with sturdy flowers and foliage – roses are excellent – as plants that have fragile and hollow stems can easily be damaged if held too tightly.

All the plant material chosen for this hand-tie is green, forming a monochromatic colour scheme. Using tints and hues of a single colour in an arrangement often produces a very strong visual effect, because it focuses attention on the different textures in the design. This hand-tied bouquet demonstrates this well: the eye is drawn to the individual shapes and textures of each element. Here I have chosen plant material that is wild and natural – reminiscent of the original sheaves of corn with which the age-old hand-tie technique originated. For a successful result, start by using the straighter stems and the seed heads in the centre, adding the trailing foliage around the outside of the arrangement.

Ingredients

Grasses
Wild oats (*Avena fatua*)
Millet grass
(*Pennisetum setaceum*)
Hare's tail (*Lagurus ovatus*)
Wheat (*Triticum aestivim*)
Heath sedge
(*Carex flacca* 'Schreb')
Barley (*Hordeum*)

Other foliage & seed heads
Carthamus seed heads
(*Carthamus tinctorius*)
Poppy seed heads
(*Papaver orientale*)
Snake grass (*Equisetum hyemale*)
Dill (*Anethum graveolens*)
Amaranthus (*Amaranthus hypochondriacus* 'Viridis')

Classical urn arrangement

This is a classic pedestal arrangement – a formal design that is appropriate for grand and very special occasions or locations. This kind of composition is suited to the foyers of hotels and prestigious establishments or to make a statement for weddings and celebrations – a large design like this will be noticed by everyone. An urn of flowers on a pedestal raises the flowers above eye level to create impact.

I prefer to use heavy bases that are very stable and able to take the considerable weight of an urn when filled with flowers and water. The placing of a display like this has a crucial effect on its impact and will also dictate the mechanics you will need. Pedestal arrangements are generally designed to be front facing (placed against a wall); three-quarters, when they can be seen at the sides but are mainly front facing; or to be placed in the middle of a room, when they will be seen from around.

Ingredients

Flowers & foliage
Flowering privet (*Ligustrum*)
Miniature date palm
(*Phoenix roebelenii*)
Variegated trailing ivy (*Hedera*)
Delphiniums
Agapanthus or African lilies
(*Agapanthus africanus*)
Foxtail lilies (*Eremurus*)
Snowberries
(*Symphoricarpos albus*)
Onion heads (*Allium giganteum*)
Chimney bellflowers
(*Campanula pyramidalis*)
Arum lilies
(*Zantedeschia aethiopica*)
Two potted hydrangeas
(*Hydrangea macrophylla*)
Amaryllis (*Hippeastrum*)
'Casablanca' lilies

Other materials
Heavy urn
Plastic bucket to line urn
Roll of 2in (5cm) wire mesh
8 extension tubes or cones
8 bamboo canes
Wire and tape

Zantedeschia aethiopica 'Tinkerbell'

1 This reconstituted marble urn was made to look antique by rubbing grey and brown emulsion paint into the stone with an old rag, and flicking and brushing paint into the crevices with an old toothbrush. Place a bucket inside the urn and wedge it in firmly so that the container is stable. Take some large-gauge (2in/5cm) wire mesh (this makes inserting the stems easier) and loosely crumple it into a ball to fit inside the bucket.

2 A large pedestal display – this one measured 6.5ft (2m) in height once it was finished – should be placed at or above eye level. Select plant material with long stems to give height to the arrangement; you can also use plastic florist's cones or tubes to lengthen stems (see Techniques, page 174). Attach several cones to bamboo canes, securing them with wire and tape, and place these at different angles into the wire mesh.

5 Next add the snowberries and the allium heads. Fill in with a little more foliage and add a few more ivy trails to all sides of the arrangement so that the edge of the container is softened. The flowers you have added so far have all been spires and so have added to the height of the design. Tall flowers such as these are perfect for large-scale displays like this. Next you will need to add the "fillers" and some flowers of other shapes to complete the arrangement.

6 Place short-stemmed flowers, such as the chimney bellflowers and the arum lilies, into the cones. Take two potted hydrangeas and insert two or three canes through the holes in the bottom of the flower pots. If there are no holes in the base of the pots then remove them completely and insert the canes directly into the peat moss. Place the canes supporting the hydrangeas into the middle of the arrangement, so that their large heads will act as the focal flowers. Add the hollow-stemmed amaryllis. Insert canes into their stems to prevent them from drooping (see pages 178–9). Finally, fill in any gaps with foxtail and 'Casablanca' lilies and make sure that the display has an even density throughout.

3 Take the flowering privet and large fronds of date palm to establish the outline of the arrangement, and place swags of trailing ivy over the rim of the urn. Most importantly, don't be afraid to make the outline large. The plant material must be in proportion with the size of the urn; as a general guideline, the finished arrangement should be at least one and a half times the height of the container (including the plinth if there is one).

4 Arrange the longer-stemmed flowers such as the delphiniums, agapanthus, and foxtail lilies. As usual, you should condition your flowers by leaving them in a bucket of nutrient-enriched water for several hours before you begin to add them to the display.

7 When you have finished the arrangement, stand well back so that you can admire it from a distance and see if the shape and overall look is pleasing to the eye. If you notice any gaps, readjust the flowers or add some new ones to fill the holes. Finally, carefully fill the bucket with lukewarm water mixed with flower food, using a watering can. Make sure that the water level is as high as possible, as a large mixed arrangement like this will quickly drink up the water.

Creating a large arrangement

- Decide on the location of the finished display and whether it will be front facing, three-quarters, or visible from all sides.

- Choose bold plant material to suit the size of the arrangement. It is possible to order many varieties of flowers that have stems 2½–3ft (80–90cm) long and there are also lots of long branches available.

- Take time to ensure that your mechanics are suitable for the size of your envisaged arrangement and that they will not let you down. Two-inch (5cm) wire mesh is excellent for such large-scale displays.

- Continually stand well back from your arrangement so that you can keep an eye on the shape as it progresses.

- Make sure that your plant material trails downward over the edge of the container – this will give the arrangement depth and movement.

Basket of greens

Foliage plays an integral part in my floral work. In most cases the foliage is the material that forms the background from which the flowers will stand out. It is also important for introducing structure, shape, and balance to a display. However, in all seasons there is enough variety of foliage available to enable the floral designer to create an arrangement using foliage on its own.

This arrangement uses a simple combination of deciduous and evergreen foliages – chosen for their different textures, colours, and forms – with just three focal flowers of anthuriums. It is an excellent example of an arrangement with movement – the whole basket looks brimming with energy. The rhythm in this design has been created by using the different types of foliage to move the eye across the arrangement. The gently curved and flowing lines of the foliage give a very natural appearance to the whole arrangement.

This arrangement is very natural and wild, and the old metal egg basket I have used here makes an appropriate container. Fit a bowl or other water-holding container inside the outer one and tuck pieces of sphagnum moss between the two.

For an assembly such as this I prefer to hand-tie the material before placing into the water – a hand-tie is quicker to achieve, I have more control over its assembly, and it is easier to keep the vase clean. (*See* Techniques, page 177, for more information on creating hand-ties.) As a general principle, I try where possible to arrange flowers and foliage in water rather than in foam. Plant material lasts longer this way and it enables me to change the water, giving the display a greater chance of looking fresher for longer.

Ingredients

Flowers & foliage
Sphagnum moss
(*Sphagnum auriculatum*)
Anthuriums
(*Anthurium andraeanum* 'Simba')
Blue gum eucalyptus
(*Eucalyptus globulus*)
Seeded eucalyptus
(*Eucalyptus polanthemos*)
Spiraea (*Spiraea* × *vanhouttei*
'Bridal Wreath')
Pittosporum
(*Pittosporum tenuifolium*)
Copper beech
(*Fagus sylvatica* f. *purpurea*)
Sorbus (*Sorbus aria* 'Lutescens')
Amaranthus
(*Amaranthus hypochondriacus*)

Other materials
Old metal egg basket or other
stout container
Bowl or other waterproof
container to fit the above

Primrose pot

Simply arranged flowers will never go out of style. I have been making little pots of flowers like this for all sorts of occasions over the last fifteen years and they look just as cute and beguiling as ever, no matter what the season or the surroundings in which they are displayed. If you cover a simple jar or glass with leaves, the whole arrangement will have a lovely natural glow and the container will be in sympathy with the flowers. Any glossy leaves will work, which makes this design very versatile. This arrangement uses lots of small delicate spring flowers, such as hellebores, miniature roses, and primroses. Although these flowers are beautiful in their own right, they are quite tiny and tend to get lost in a larger mixed bunch: arranging them in groups helps to give them greater impact. When you are creating a hand-tie of small flowers like these, it helps if you start by bunching the flowers into groups of one variety, securing each small bunch with raffia, before you begin to create the larger, spiral hand-tie. This technique can be used for all sorts of small delicate flowers, such as snowdrops, violets and forget-me-nots.

To create this simple arrangement you need to cover an old jam jar or glass tumbler in double-sided tape. Remove the stalks from the galax leaves and the outer layer of paper from the tape and attach the leaves around the edge of the jar or glass. Tie with some bear grass around the centre of the container and fill it with water.

To make the posy, first clean all the lower stems of the flowers so that no leaves will be left below the waterline to pollute the water. Lay the flowers out in groups and bind the smaller ones, such as the primroses, into a neat group, tying them together with raffia. Begin the hand-tie with a bunch of miniature roses, then continue to add flowers in groups slightly at angles to the central bunch and to the left. Turn the posy as you add bunches of hellebores, miniature narcissi, and ixia. Use the larger achillea and dill as single heads around the edges, then add a few short branches of broom to soften the edges. Tie the posy, trim the stems, and fit it snugly into your leafed container.

Ingredients

Flowers & foliage
Galax leaves (*Galax aphylla*)
Bunch of bear grass
(*Xerophyllum asphodeloides*)
Primroses (*Primula vulgaris*)
Miniature roses
(*Rosa micro* 'Lemon')
Christmas roses
(*Helleborus niger*)
Miniature narcissi
(*Narcissus* 'Liberty Bells')
Ixia (*Ixia* 'Spotlight')
Achillea (*Achillea filipendulina*
'Cream Perfection')
Dill (*Anethum graveolens*)
Broom (*Genista*)

Other materials
Jam jar or glass tumbler
Double-sided tape
Raffia

Anethum graveolens 'Lumina'

Sunflower and lily trailing arrangement

If you are decorating a room that has a fireplace, then the mantelpiece is an excellent place for a flower arrangement. Mantelpieces are often quite narrow and usually fairly high up, and so they provide a platform for a floral display at the perfect height for your guests to enjoy it. I love the sort of droopy designs in which there is as much plant material dangling down over the mantelpiece as there is interest above it. Obviously you will need to consider whether you plan to have a fire in the grate when you are deciding on the proportions for the design. I like to create such arrangements on site so that I can achieve a perfect fit for the mantelpiece.

Ingredients

Flowers & foliage

Northern American pin oak
(*Quercus ellipsoidalis*)
Sweet chestnut
(*Castanea sativa*)
Ivy trails (*Hedera helix*)
Crab apples
(*Malus* 'Red Sentinel')
Amaranthus (*Amaranthus caudatus* 'Green Tails')
Asclepias (*Asclepias tuberosa* 'Gay Butterfly')
Euphorbia (*Euphorbia fulgens* 'Yellow River')
Lilies
(*Lilium* 'Golden Splendour')
Sunflowers (*Helianthus annuus* 'Teddy Bear')
Dill (*Anethum graveolens*)

Other materials

Long basket window box with zinc liner
7 blocks of florist's foam
Florist's tape

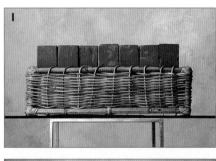

1 I prefer to make trailing displays like this in window boxes. This basket has a zinc liner, but I often use ordinary outdoor terracotta boxes, spray-painted and lined with a plastic window box. Fill the box with blocks of soaked florist's foam, placing them on end and taping them in place.

2 Using this number of foam blocks means that you have a wide area in which to place plant material – at the front, allowing some to trail downward, and at the back, reaching upright against the chimney breast.

Begin with the foliage and crab apples, making sure that you add them right at the back of the foam as well as at the front, so that the arrangement is structurally balanced and will not fall forward. A mixture of different types of foliage is always good – some trailing, some upright in habit, and some busy and dense. Next add the trailing flowers: the amaranthus, asclepias, and euphorbia. The old-fashioned trumpet lilies are multi-headed and need lots of space: arrange them at different heights and depths throughout the greenery. You are then ready to add the dominant sunflowers. Finally, use the green dill to fill any gaps.

Helianthus annuus 'Teddy Bear'

Autumn in a vase

Choosing a successful combination of flowers is one of the most daunting tasks for the amateur flower arranger. Whether or not a design works will depend, in large part, on two main factors: the colour choice and the shape of the flowers. This massed vase design is a good example of a successful combination of flower colours and shapes. Here the tone of the display was set by the complementary rings of colours on the vase, which the flowers were chosen to echo. Using lots of colours of a similar tone can make a display look very busy; the addition of a deep rich foliage – I used Cotinus coggygria *'Purpurea' here – will help harmonize the whole. I also like to add a touch of lime green to multicoloured arrangements: here the bupleurum and amaranthus catch the light and enhance the other flowers. Varying the shapes of the flowers is particularly important in a larger arrangement such as this. Tall, elegant ones, such as red-hot pokers and calla lilies, are excellent for creating the outline shape, while in this display the spiky arachnis orchids create lines and the large, round gerbera heads act as focal flowers.*

To create a vase arrangement like this, select five groups of flowers and about five types of foliage, or "fillers" as florists and flower arrangers tend to call them. Lay them out in neat piles and remove all the lower leaves so that the stems are clear and will not create bacteria in the water. After thoroughly cleaning the vase, begin to arrange the bushy foliage – in this case the cotinus, viburnum berries, and rudbeckia. Add each piece of foliage into the centre so that all the stems radiate from that central point. Next add in the spiky amaranthus in red and green and a few spikes of the fluffy bupleurum. You are now ready to begin the outline of the design, using the red hot pokers and the calla lilies. As this is a round arrangement it is important to work on all sides, so keep turning the vase, continuing to place material into the middle. Use the dendrobium orchids to create lines radiating from the centre and then add some brightly coloured tansies to lighten any gaps and fill the display. Finally, add the gerberas at different heights and depths.

Ingredients

Flowers & foliage
Cotinus (*Cotinus coggygria* 'Purpurea')
Viburnum berries (*Viburnum opulus*)
Rudbeckia (*Rudbeckia hirta*)
Spiky amaranthus (*Amaranthus hypochondriacus* 'Pigmy Viridis')
Bupleurum (*Bupleurum griffithi*)
Red-hot pokers (*Kniphofia* 'Royal Standard')
Calla lilies (*Zantedeschia* 'Florex Gold')
Orchids (*Arachnis* 'Maggie Oei')
Tansies (*Tanacetum vulgare* 'Isla Gold')
Gerberas (*Gerbera* 'Tiramisu')

Arachnis 'Maggie Oei'

Rose urn

This is the most classic of arrangements – one type of flower and one variety of foliage in a very traditional container. Arrangements like this are the floral equivalent of "the little black dress" – always looking good and gracing a range of locations. For such a display to be successful, you should use only the very best garden roses in prime condition.

Ingredients

Flowers & foliage
Mixed varieties of garden roses
Ivy trails with berries
(*Hedera helix*)

Other materials
Table urn
2 blocks of florist's foam

1

1 Arrange the two blocks of soaked florist's foam in the table urn, allowing a generous height – about 2in (5cm) – of foam above the top of the container. This will enable you to add flowers at all angles, including some at right angles to the edge of the container. Begin by adding the ivy trails around the edge of the urn, always radiating the stems from the central point in the arrangement. Allow some of the ivy trails to fall over the rim.

2

2 When most of the foam is covered, begin to add the flowers, starting with the sprays of roses with the smallest heads or the tightest buds. Move the urn around as you work so that you are adding flowers from all sides while maintaining a flow of material from the central point of the display. Add the fuller and larger roses into the main focal areas of the arrangement and mix up the colours to give a lovely natural feel to the design.

Ranunculus arrangement

Often clients find it difficult to describe what they like and need some visual aids to help them explain their preferences. Sometimes an arrangement will trigger an emotional response that will help them understand what they appreciate about it. Personally, I am happiest with designs like this one that look effortless and natural. Achieving a good design is not only about combining elements within the work to great effect, but also taking into consideration external factors, such as the setting and the purpose for which the display is intended. The materials, style, and location should all complement one another and work together to create a harmonious whole.

Balance is a very important principle in floral design – actual and visual balance. Actual or physical balance simply means that the arrangement is stable. Visual balance is more subjective and personal. However, it is generally agreed that all arrangements should have an area that is perceived to contain the most interest. In a visually balanced design, plant materials will be arranged around an imaginary vertical or horizontal axis so that the eye is drawn equally to both sides.

To achieve a well-balanced, all-round vase arrangement, place plant material so that it radiates from the centre and has equal weight on all sides. Smaller, more delicate flowers and foliage create the outline, while larger, heavier flowers are used for the bulk and centre of the arrangement. In this design, the marigolds and ranunculus balance each other, while the asclepias, hebe and *Alchemilla mollis* lend movement and softness to the round shape of the focal flowers. Visual balance has been created, even though the arrangement is not symmetrical.

Ingredients

Flowers & foliage
Marigolds (*Calendula officinalis*)
Ranunculus (*Ranunculus* 'Apricot')
Asclepias
(*Asclepias tuberosa* 'Beatrix')
Hebe (*Hebe cupressoides*)
Lady's mantle (*Alchemilla mollis*)
Bupleurum (*Bupleurum griffithii*)

"Ice" rose topiary

This is a very simple design and visually very effective. In a tall, thin vase, like the one shown here, it makes a great table centrepiece, but the same design can be translated into a much wider vase to create a larger and equally striking display. The petals and Cellophane last quite well – up to five days, or even longer if the conditions are not too hot and the vase is away from direct sunlight. Obviously this is a difficult design to transport, and it benefits from being created in situ.

Ingredients

Roses (*Rosa*)
20 stems of each of the following:
'Sphinx'
'Black Bacarra'
'Milva'
'Lemon and lime'
'Grand Prix'
'Athena'

Other materials
Cellophane
Tall (30in/1m), thin flared vase
15in (38cm) diameter florist's foam ball

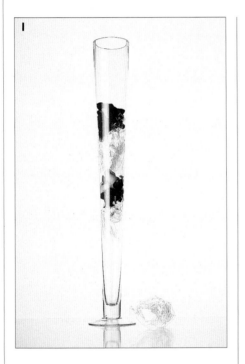

1 I have used Cellocoup – a type of Cellophane – for this design. Cellocoup is stronger than ordinary Cellophane, and so is ideal for use here, though the standard variety will suffice. Put alternate bundles of scrunched up Cellophane and small handfuls of mixed-colour petals in the stem of the vase. You will need petals from about six flower heads for this. Fill the vase with water to keep the petals fresh. Submerge the florist's foam ball in water until it is fully saturated and the air bubbles cease to rise.

2 Place the foam ball on a raised surface, such as a small cylinder vase, so that you can work on all sides of it. Cut off the rose heads, leaving a ¾in (2cm) stem, and angle them into the ball. Mix the colours to create a patchwork of colour. Remember to work on all sides so that the roses all radiate from the centre. Balance the finished ball on top of the vase and spray it with a fine mister .

A florist's foam ball makes a perfect sphere of flowers, and for one this size you will need about 120 heads (more if they are in bud or small). For a cheaper alternative, hand-tie a semi-circle of fifty to sixty roses, with or without foliage.

Rosa 'Ambiance'

Sunflower explosion

Grasses are very much in fashion, both in the garden and in the vase. The relationship between trends in garden design and those in flower arranging is very close. Any trip to a garden show will give you ideas and inspiration, and if you are lucky enough to visit a big national show, such as those of the Royal Horticultural Society in the UK, you will soon get a feel for what is in vogue. I have also found great inspiration in the way some garden designers use plants – Beth Chatto's natural ecological garden near Elmstead Market in England is one of my favourites. I also admire the planting of the English designer Dan Pearson and the Dutch landscape gardener Piet Oudolf. Piet's work is instantly recognizable, with its vibrant hues and structural grasses.

The choice of foliage is central to my work: as well as employing foliage to support the central flowers, I also use it to help set a mood and to enhance the overall colour scheme of an arrangement. Grasses also create movement in a floral design, in much the same way as they do in a garden. Here the long grasses complement the density and roundness of the flowers and move your eye across the design.

Van Gogh's *Sunflowers* were on my mind when I began this design – its starting point was the fluffy yellow 'Teddy Bear' double sunflowers painted by him. An old Provençal olive pot makes the perfect container – slightly worn and shabby like the banksia and protea flowers and in matching tones so that it won't overpower the flowers.

To arrange flowers in a vase like this, start with the busy foliage – in this case the red robin – using it to begin to build up the structure. Next add the flax and the reeds. You are now ready for the flowers: start with the sunflowers, then add the proteas and banksias. Leave the eucomis and chrysanthemums until last: because their stems are slightly weaker, you will need to place them carefully and avoid disturbing them too much. Finally, add bunches of zebra grass all around the arrangement.

Ingredients

Flowers & foliage
Red robin
(*Photinia* x *fraseri* 'Red Robin')
New Zealand flax leaves
(*Phormium tenax* 'Variegatum')
Screw pine reeds
(*Pandanus odoratissimus*)
Sunflowers
(*Helianthus* 'Teddy Bear')
Proteas (*Protea repens*)
Banksia (*Banksia ashbeyi*)
Steel grass (*Xanthorrhoea preissii* 'Black Boy')
Pineapple flowers
(*Eucomis bicolor*)
Chrysanthemums
(*Chrysanthemum* 'Tom Pierce')
Zebra grass
(*Miscanthus sinensis* 'Zebrinus')

Hand-tied calla lilies

The perfect spiral has been created using these sculptural calla or arum lilies. Because the stems of these lilies are so clean, they create a wonderfully architectural shape as they twist in the same direction. You can also vary the angle at which they are placed into the design. The trumpet heads are generally positioned so that their tips are facing the outside of the posy to create this mushroom shape, and each flower is placed into the bunch at an angle of about fifteen degrees from the vertical central flower.

Calla lilies are popular flowers because of their very sculptural shape, which makes them versatile for many kinds of floral design. The rich- and dark-coloured varieties are particularly prized by top floral designers, and can always command a high price on the world flower scene. Only the weaker colours, such as the pale yellow and dusty pink, and the shorter specimens are generally available at a more affordable price. Bouquets of this simple shape are a favourite with brides all over the world, especially when they are created using white calla lilies.

There is no preparation required to make this hand-tie because the stems are already straight and clean. Using these lilies is the ultimate way to test your hand-tying skills: if the bouquet is perfectly balanced it will stand on its own stems like this one. Balance of any hand-tie will be achieved if you continue to turn the flowers a quarter turn every time you add five or so stems of flowers. This will mean that you are continually working on all side of the design. Practice makes perfect – before long you will be able to do this in your sleep!

Ingredients

Calla lilies (*Zantedeschia*)
10 'Mango'
10 'Yellow Queen'
10 'Golden Affair'
10 'Pink Persuasion'
10 'Little Jim'
10 'Little Dream'

Other materials
Thick cord to tie

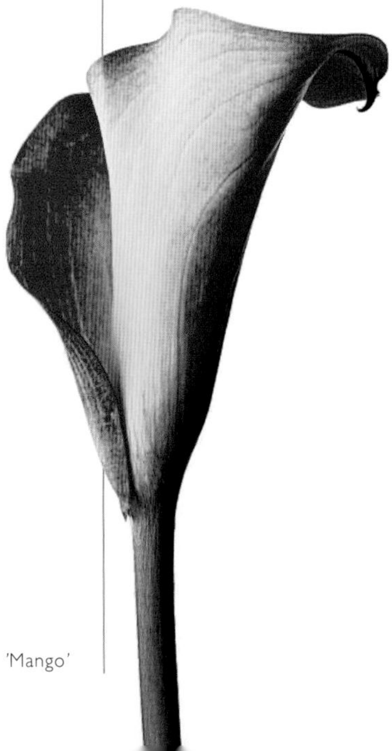

Zantedeschia 'Mango'

Lily and fruit centrepiece

The botanists who gathered lilies from all over the world have bequeathed us a rich heritage. One of my favourite lilies, Lilium regale, was discovered comparatively recently (in 1937) in western China by the British plant-hunter Dr Ernest Wilson. It was growing, he wrote, "not in twos and threes but in hundreds, in thousands, aye, in tens of thousands." He sent some to a British nursery where they were tested and found to do very well in the British soil. Quantities of these bulbs reached the USA at about the same time. These spectacular lilies will grow to 3ft (1m) tall and can carry as many as fourteen trumpets on each stem. Their scent is divine and their wine and pink markings are most attractive. The centres of these lilies are almost buttercup yellow in colour, and it is from this strain that the golden yellow 'Royal Gold' variety was developed.

1 Fill a straight-sided glass bowl with a selection of mouthwatering fruit. I used papaya, black cherries with their stems still attached, red-currants, and strawberries. Make sure that the fruit is in prime condition.

Ingredients

Flowers & foliage
Senecio (*Senecio*)
Dill (*Anethum graveolens*)
Viburnum berries (*Viburnum*)
Rudbeckia
Roses (*Rosa* 'Peer Gynt' and 'Leonardis')
Dark red astilbe (*Astilbe*)
'Royal Gold' lilies (*Lilium regale*)

Other materials
Straight-sided glass bowl
Selection of attractive fruit
Plastic-backed florist's foam ring to fit the diameter of your bowl

Astilbe

2 Soak a florist's foam ring the diameter of your bowl in warm water and flower food. Cut the senecio into small sprigs about 2–3in (5–7.5cm) long and cover the ring with them.

3 Add the foliage to provide interest and texture. The green dill lightens the overall colour and the viburnum berries give a nice droop to the lower line of the arrangement. Next add the rudbeckia.

4 Cut the stems of the roses, astilbe, and lilies to about 2–3 in (5–7.5cm) long. Position the roses and astilbe throughout the display.

Finally (below), add the lilies, again arranging them throughout.

'Leonardis' rose Victorian posy

Every so often a new variety comes onto the flower market and takes centre stage. When the brown bicolour 'Leonardis' rose arrived on the scene in the latter part of the 1990s, it quickly attained superstar status and was the "one" favoured by brides, event planners, and lovers. The new colour was intriguing and captivating; its deep rust colour presented floral designers with a new palette to play with and it was inspirational in lots of new floral designs. Professional and amateur florists are constantly being presented with new varieties and this leads to new fashions and styles in floral design. This new brown-coloured rose looks great with textured plant material, and berries and seed heads began to enjoy prominence featured alongside it. Hypericum and rudbeckia were still seasonal at the time, but have since become more available, the former developing into an all-year-round staple. The deep rust colour made the shades of peach seem stronger and more tempting, and it also worked very well with other softer pastels such as beige. Before long the new rose was everywhere. Alas, long before it appeared in the buckets at supermarkets it had lost its cult status.

This posy is based on the Victorian idea of using different flowers arranged in concentric circles. Traditionally these were very ordered arrangements, made by wiring the flowers into either a posy or an arrangement of moss, which would give the designer more control over the order and exact placement of the flowers. However, I like the idea of taking a formal design such as this and then arranging it very simply and naturally in a spiral hand-tie. Start with a a central rose and then add the other plant material in rings, finishing with the cordata leaves to edge the posy. These flowers are still on their natural stems so can drink water freely, which means that the posy will last much longer. One advantage of this kind of formal design is that by being massed into rings, the plant material gains visual strength. This allows you to put together flowers and foliage that would not combine easily in a massed posy.

Ingredients

Roses (*Rosa*)
'Leonardis'
'Versillea'

Other flowers & foliage
Hebe (*Hebe cupressoides* 'Boughton Dome')
Skimmia
(*Skimmia japonica* 'Rubella')
Arabian chincherinchees
(*Ornithogalum arabicum*)
Cordata leaves

Other materials
Length of florist's tie

Hand-tie in an urn

To create a full and rounded pedestal arrangement, I like to use the method of hand-tying rather than arranging flowers in the conventional way. Hand-tying allows you greater control over the shape of the design, enabling you to create a display with a lovely full effect, like the one shown here. Although in theory you are limited by how much you can hold in your hand, you will find that if you are careful, and rest the bunch on your work bench, you can actually manage a lot of plant material. Another advantage of this method is that it helps you to ensure that the flower stems are very clean, which will mean that your arrangement lasts longer. Large hand-ties are great for contract work or gifts because they can be kept tied up, enabling the client or recipient to remove dead flower heads, keep the container clean, refresh the water, and even recut the stems, all of which will help prolong the life of the display. A hand-tied bunch can also be kept secure in transit.

Ingredients

Flowers & foliage
15 pink roses (*Rosa* 'Diplomat')
10 delphiniums
(*Delphinium* 'Yvonne')
10 pink snowberries
(*Symphoricarpos* 'Pink Pearl')
7 lilies (*Lilium* 'Medusa')
10 roses (*Rosa* 'Eden')
Bunch of viburnum berries
(*Viburnum lantana*)
10 stems of dill
(*Anethum graveolens*)
10 bells of Ireland
(*Molucella laevis*)
10 purple lisianthus (*Eustoma russellianum* 'Kyoto Purple')
10 ivy trails (*Hedera helix*)

Other materials
Wired florist's tie
Plastic bucket
(Moss) urn
(Moss) plinth

Lilium 'Romanesco'

I Clean the lower stems of all your plant material. Choose a flower with a straight stem as your central one – I have started with a stem of black-berried *Viburnum lantana*. Holding this first stem in your left hand (if you are right-handed), add the next piece of plant material – in this case a lily. Holding the growing bunch in your left hand leaves your right hand free to lift material and trim stems as necessary. Add each new stem almost at a right angle to the left of the previous one.

2 After you have added about five stems, you will need to twist the bunch in your hand. Do this by simply taking hold of the bunch with your right hand and moving it around in your left so that you are working on a new side. If you do not do this every time you have added five to seven stems, you will end up with a linear shape rather than a lovely rounded bouquet. Mix up the plant material as you progress so that you achieve variety.

3 Continue to build up the bunch so that all the stems fan out like a sheaf. Trim the stems a little as you proceed to keep the bunch manageable, and remember to mix in foliage as well flowers to give it shape and help hold the design together. As the bouquet gets bigger, increase the angle at which you add new flowers and foliage so that the arrangement is rounded and full.

The art of making a large hand-tie

The best way to success with hand tying is to make sure that you clean all the stems. As well as helping to prevent pollution in the water, this leaves the binding point clear and makes it easier to achieve a good neat spiral bunch. A good variety of plant material – foliage as well as flowers – is essential for making a large hand-tie. Select many different flower shapes, including fillers, round shapes, spires, and other shapes (see also pages 14–17). The following are all good for large hand-ties:

4 When you have used all the plant material, tie the bunch at the point at which you have been holding it – the binding point. I like to use wired florist's tie (bind wire), which is made from wire bound with paper string, as it is stronger and creates a tighter tie than ordinary garden string. If your bouquet is well balanced it will stand as shown above. Trim the stems to the same length, cutting them on the diagonal to increase their capacity to take up water. Make sure that the stems are completely clear of any leaves as these will create harmful bacteria in the water, which will kill the flowers prematurely.

Place the bucket in the urn so that it fits snugly, wiring or taping it into place as necessary, then fill it with water mixed with flower food.

5 Place the hand-tie into the bucket, then add a few trails of ivy to soften the line of the container. Top the water right up to the edge of the container so that everything can have a long drink. If the urn is for a special occasion, then I would release the tie so that the plant material is a little more relaxed. If the arrangement is for a contract vase, then keep the bunch tied up, as this will be invaluable for maintenance.

Fillers:

*   Dill (*Anethum graveolens*), lisianthus (*Eustoma russellianum*), gypsophila, solidaster

Round shapes:

*   Gerberas, standard chrysanthemums, roses, peonies

Spire shapes:

*   Bells of Ireland (*Moluccella laevis*), monkshood (*Aconitum*), delphiniums

Stars and other shapes:

*   Nerines, lilies, agapanthus

Eustoma russellianum 'Mariachi Pink'

Strawberries and cream

I love to use fruit in my flower arrangements, especially when it is plentiful, cheap, and in season. This design makes the most of inexpensive seasonal summer flowers and herbs, and includes some strawberries for more texture and colour. As a general rule, I only use fruit with flowers for a special occasion, when the longevity of the flowers is not of prime importance, as the addition of any fruit and vegetables will shorten the life of the flowers and foliage. All natural materials produce an ageing hormone called ethylene gas, and ripe soft fruit such as strawberries, particularly when they have been pierced to place them in the foam, will pose a risk to the longevity of an arrangement. Ethylene gas is also produced when a plant or flower starts to decompose, so remember to remove any plant material that has passed its best in order to give the rest of the arrangement the chance to survive longer. Positioning the display in a well-ventilated room will help to disperse the gas. Ideally the environment should also be cool and insect-free. With such precautions in place, I would expect an arrangement like this to last about five days. The fruit will inevitably start to deteriorate before the flowers fade.

This classic topiary arrangement is very simple to create. First soak a jumbo block of florist's foam in water until the bubbles stop rising (indicating that the foam is full of water). Trim the base of the foam with a knife and fit it into a watertight ceramic pot, then sculpt it into the shape you wish to make the topiary display. Clip the flowers and foliage so that the stems are about 1 in (2.5cm) long, then begin to add them to the foam, one type at a time. Using herbs in a summer arrangement always adds fragrance, and I love the blue-grey foliage of the 'Jackman's Blue' variety of rue. In this arrangement, I started with the rue, then added the border carnations. Finally, spear each strawberry with a wooden cocktail stick through the hull and stick these into the foam. I deliberately chose to leave the hulls intact and to position them on the outside, in order to provide more texture and give the arrangement additional interest.

Ingredients

Flowers, foliage & fruit
Rue (*Ruta graveolens* 'Jackman's Blue')
Border carnations (pinks) (*Dianthus* 'Haytor' and 'Doris')
Strawberries (*Fragaria* hybrids)

Other materials
Jumbo block of florist's foam
Watertight ceramic pot
Wooden cocktail sticks

Dianthus 'Haytor'

Peony arrangement

Travellers to China in the 18th century reported that they had seen a new flower, like a gigantic rose but without the thorns. They were describing peonies. These spectacularly beautiful flowers, which have had a long history as cut flowers, were frequently combined with other exquisite blooms in the work of the Dutch flower artists. But in my opinion they look best simply arranged in a low bowl, where they seem to float among their own foliage. The best peonies for cut flowers and fragrance are the bright-pink, scented varieties such as 'Dr Alexander Fleming' and 'Monsieur Jules Elie', the pale-pink, fragrant 'Lady Alexandra Duff' and 'Shirley Temple', and the white 'Duchesse de Nemours', 'Gardenia', and 'Charlie's White'. I also recommend the red 'Karl Rosenfield', and the mid-pink 'Sarah Bernhardt', both of which, although not known for their scent, are very long lasting and their rich colours work well in large pedestal displays and bridal bouquets. Commercial peonies are cut first thing in the morning, while still in tight bud, and plunged directly into water. Kept in a cool place, peonies will survive happily for two weeks, making them a very popular summer bloom.

Peonies have a very classic appearance and so are ideal for simple classic arrangements like this. I have used a mixture of peony varieties so that the look is natural, and have added only a few spikes of lady's mantle (*Alchemilla mollis*) to liven up the colours of the peonies and give some movement and outline to the arrangement. Peonies are very popular with florists because they are so adaptable – they look just as happy in a cottage setting as they do in a cathedral; they look good in a natural uncontrived arrangement, as here, but they can also be dressed up to look the part in a formal arrangement for a grand ball or wedding. I love to use them with early spring cherry blossom, delphiniums, foxgloves, stocks, lilies, lilacs, and guelder roses for late spring weddings.

Ingredients

Peonies (*Paeonia*)
'Sarah Bernhardt'
'Dr Alexander Fleming'
'Duchesse de Nemours'
'Shirley Temple'
'China Rose'

Other flowers & foliage
Lady's mantle (*Alchemilla mollis*)

Country basket

If you grow flowers in your garden then you have an ideal source of material for making informal arrangements. When you pick blooms straight from the garden, you must always give them a long drink of nutrient-enriched water before you start arranging, otherwise they will soon begin to wilt and look tired. (All cut flowers will look fresher for longer if they have been properly conditioned before arranging.)

You should avoid wiring any plant material when creating an informal theme; instead allow the stems and flower heads to fall naturally. Seasonal blossom and all kinds of flowering foliage and herbs are suitable for informal arranging.

Ingredients

Flowers & foliage
Dill (*Anethum graveolens*)
Marjoram (*Origanum*)
Soapwort (*Saponaria*)
Mallow (*Malva*)
Masterwort (*Astrantia*)
Cow parsley (*Anthriscus sylvestris*)
Mock orange
(*Philadelphus coronarius*)
Poppy (*Papaver*)
Love-lies-bleeding
(*Amaranthus caudatus*)
Globe artichoke (*Cynara scolymus*)
Lupin (*Lupinus*)
Stock (*Matthiola*)
Mullein (*Verbascum*)
Valerian (*Valeriana*)
Cirsium (*Cirsium*)
Eupatorium
Scabious (*Scabiosa*)
Milkweed (*Euphorbia*)
Achillea
Phlomis
Loosestrife (*Lysimachia*)

Dock seed head (*Rumex*)
Oats (*Avena sativa*)
Millet (*Millum*)
Rue (*Ruta graveolens*)
Copper beech (*Fagus sylvatica purpurea*)
Giant reeds and ornamental grass
(e.g. *Arundo donax*)
Hosta (*Hosta* 'August Moon')

Other materials
Plain wooden, terracotta, or earthenware container
Bucket
Large-gauge wire mesh
Crumpled paper, straw, or moss

I Choose a suitably simple container for an informal arrangement like this. I used a 19th-century bran tub, but a plain earthenware pot, a terracotta vase, or perhaps a basket or wooden trug would be equally appropriate. If the container you have chosen for your arrangement is not watertight you will need to place a bucket inside it. Take some large-gauge wire mesh and crumple it into a loose ball that will fit snugly inside the bucket, then fill the bucket with water. Wedge the bucket inside the outer container with crumpled paper, straw, or moss.

4 Continue to fill in any gaps with flowers of different colours and make sure that all the flower heads are facing forward. You must singe the ends of the poppy stems before adding them to the display (see Techniques, page 176) otherwise their sap will contaminate the water. Use the hanging love-lies-bleeding and the masterwort to give the display shape and movement.

2 Select a handful of various different types of foliage and place them grouped together into the container. Although the taller grasses and dock seed heads will be eye-catching, some of the smaller grasses will look flimsy and will hardly be visible unless you bunch them together into a sheaf to give them as much visual impact as possible.

3 Establish the outline of the arrangement with white flowers such as soapwort, mallow, masterwort, cow parsley, and mock orange. How and where you place your flowers is a matter of instinct and preference, but the whole arrangement should look spontaneous rather than contrived, so be careful not to over-arrange it.

5 This is a very natural "English cottage garden" arrangement, created early in the summer when these seasonal flowers are all at their best. This combination of colours is one of my favourites, and these flowers are also wonderfully fragrant.

Achieving an informal look

- Many different types of foliage and flowers help to create a wild and natural look.

- Drooping plant material gives the arrangement movement. Trailing love-lies-bleeding is particularly good for this.

- Sprays of flowers or branches make the arrangement more naturalistic.

- Never group flowers in an informal display – it looks too controlled. (You may need to mass some of the smaller, flimsier grasses, however.)

- Adding grasses to any arrangement will give it a more wild appearance.

- Arranging in water rather than foam helps the display look more natural.

Rosemary bowl table arrangement

By concealing a plastic pot with foliage leaves or reeds you can create a cheap and attractive container. Box, spruce, lavender, and rosemary are just a few of my favourites for this.

1 To create this arrangement you need a straight-sided, round plastic bulb bowl about 12in (30cm) in diameter. Attach some thick double-sided sticky tape to the outer edge of the bowl (I find the double-sided tape often sold as carpet tape in DIY stores is excellent for this kind of arrangement). Cut the rosemary into shorter lengths so that each stem is just taller than the bowl. Remove the outer layer of the tape so that it is sticky, then place a heavy-duty rubber band around the middle of the bowl. This will enable you to place the rosemary onto the sticky tape by stretching out the rubber band. The rubber band will help keep everything in place as you work your way around the bowl.

2 Continue placing rosemary sprigs around the bowl, then trim the rosemary so that the stems are flush with the base of the bowl and neat around the top. Tie a length of sea grass or rope over the rubber band. Cut about ¾in (2cm) off the edge of each of the blocks of soaked florist's foam and then pack out the bottom of the bowl with the off-cuts. Lay the two larger blocks on their sides in the bowl so that the foam is at least 1in (2.5cm) higher than the edge of the bowl. Pin the two blocks together with two hairpin bends made from one stem of heavy wire cut into two. Make four further pins in the same way and tape them around the base of the candle, so that you can secure it into the centre of the florist's foam.

3 Next add your foliage. Use a mixture of textures and colours and arrange pieces at different heights. Radiate each stem from the central point of the arrangement. When all the foam is covered, you can begin to add the flowers. Arrange them in groups before you begin to position them into the foam. It is a good idea to add the largest flowers first, so place the three heads of pink hydrangea around the central candle at different heights. Continue to add the flowers, using the roses in groups. Remember to rotate the bowl so that you work on all sides evenly to create a lovely rounded effect. Cut the cymbidium orchid into four pieces so that you can position it evenly throughout. When the arrangement is complete, cut away the rubber band and top up the bowl with water mixed with flower food.

Ingredients

Flowers & foliage
20 stems of rosemary
(*Rosmarinus officinalis*)
7 stems of hypericum
(*Hypericum* 'Jade')
Bunch of ivy berries
(*Hedera helix*)
5 stems of senecio
(*Senecio greyii*)
5 stems of black ligature berries
(*Ligature vulgare*)
3 stems of cotinus (*Cotinus coggygria* 'Royal purple')
5 stems of snowberries
(*Symphoricarpos* 'Pink Pearl')
3 stems of pink hydrangeas
Stem of large-headed cymbidium orchid (*Cymbidium*)
4 'Aqua' roses
12 'Milano' roses
7 stems of sedum

Other materials
Plastic straight-sided bulb bowl
Double-sided sticky tape
Heavy-duty rubber band
Length of sea grass or rope
2 blocks of florist's foam
Heavy stub wires
Florist's tape
Large pillar candle

Cymbidium 'Spring'

Ivy candelabra

Candles and flowers create a great atmosphere for a party or wedding and with the right kind of metal framework nearly any kind of floral design can be achieved. I work with several metal fabricators and blacksmiths to create the structures on which I can safely create new designs.

Candelabras – whether for tables, floorstanding, or hanging – are just one of many uses for a metal base. They are very versatile – I dress them up or down for all kinds of events in diverse locations – and they are quite timeless in style. Hanging decorations are dramatic and eye-catching features. The sort of sculptural effect achieved here, using a metal frame with ivy and flowers, can look magnificent hanging in a marquee or in a double-height hall. The flowers and foliage chosen for this kind of display need to be able to cover the mechanics quickly and efficiently and to create a good shape easily. Bushy ivy foliage is ideal for this, and the roses and lilies used here add bold shapes to the design, while masterwort (Astrantia), pink achillea, and love-in-a-mist seed heads fill the arrangement and catch the candlelight.

If you are planning on hanging a floral decoration, make sure that you have a good fixing. Wet foam and flowers are much heavier than you may imagine and it is vitally important, particularly when the decoration includes candles, that it is very secure.

This design has been created using a wrought-iron frame with specially large candle cups. Tape soaked florist's foam onto the candle cups, then secure the candles in place by taping half a bamboo skewer onto the base of each one and sticking it into the centre of a foam block. Cover the foam in bushy ivy-berry foliage, trailing the ivy around the central structure of the metal candelabra and leaving it to trail. Next place the important focal flowers – the lilies and the roses – then add the filler flowers to support them, create a good shape, and lighten the arrangement.

Light the candles just before the event, but remember that draughts and air-conditioning systems can cause candles to burn down in a fraction of the manufacturer's guaranteed time.

Ingredients

Flowers & foliage
Ivy berries (*Hedera helix*)
Lilies (*Lilium* 'Imperial Gold')
Roses (*Rosa* 'Champagne' and 'Black Bacarra')
Masterwort
(*Astrantia major* 'Alba')
Achillea
(*Achillea millefolium* 'Martina')
Love-in-a-mist
(*Nigella damascena*)

Other materials
Wrought-iron candelabra with large candle cups
Florist's foam
Florist's tape
Pillar candles
Bamboo skewers

Two-tier arrangement with sweet peas

Sweet peas have been one of my favourite flowers for as long as I can remember. Among the first flowers that I grew as a child from seed, these vibrant yet delicate flowers are definitely still in my top ten. These quintessentially English garden flowers have an added bonus – not only do they make a handsome vase of flowers, but they also give an uplifting scent to your home. Even if you do not have a formal flower garden, you can make room for a few vines of sweet peas, perhaps among some vegetables – they will attract pollinating bees and other beneficial insects, as well as providing you with many sweet-scented flowers to pick.

The inspiration for this design came from the abundance of neat rows of fresh produce you can see in a kitchen garden or on an allotment at the time of year when sweet peas are in full flower. The style is very decorative and is is reminiscent of arrangements from the Victorian period in Britain, when pineapples were grown widely under glass. The pineapple is a bromeliad, like many other house plants, and became a symbol of hospitality and welcome, making it an appropriate plant to feature in an arrangement for a party or wedding.

This is a very classic arrangement which uses for its form a French wire basket. The lower basket has had spring onions attached to the outer side with raffia and the inside has been filled with leaves and then soaked moss. The lady's mantle (*Alchemilla mollis*), roses, and sweet peas have been arranged in the foam, leaving room in the centre for a heap of black cherries. The upper tier has foam covered in galax leaves and tied with ribbon, with more sweet peas and astilbes. The two tiers have been accentuated by the addition of the pineapple top, which provides a tuft of narrow pointed leaves.

When the pineapple was first discovered in central America by Columbus and his crew, it was regarded as sensational. In 1493 some fruits survived the voyage back home to Europe, and were considered nearly as great a discovery as the "New World" itself. Its unique shape became a popular motif in European art, design, and architecture.

Ingredients

Flowers & foliage
Spring onions
Lady's Mantle (*Alchemilla mollis*)
Roses (*Rosa* 'Black Beauty')
Sweet peas (*Lathyrus odoratus*)
Black cherries
Galax leaves (*Galax*)
Astilbes (*Astilbe* 'Diamant')
Pineapple top (*Ananas comosus*)

Other materials
French wire basket
Moss
Raffia
Florist's foam
Ribbon

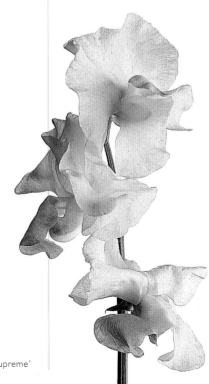

Lathyrus odoratus 'White Supreme'

Dutch "Old Master" arrangement

Art has been an enormous influence on my work, and many different styles and movements have spawned ideas for my floral designs. Among the most obvious sources of inspiration have been the Dutch and Flemish flower paintings of the 17th and 18th centuries. My first exposure to this genre was when a Flemish aunt gave my family an amateur painting that her father had done in the style of the "Old Masters". This simple picture of a vase of garden flowers was immensely colourful and moody, and portrayed flowers with a passion and sensuality that I was just beginning to relate to.

These 17th-century paintings encapsulated the fervour and reverence that exotic flowers were exciting in Europe during what became the "Golden Age" of flower painting. Crown imperials, madonna lilies, and opium poppies may be easy for us to grow or buy as cut flowers today, but many such blooms were not indigenous to Europe and had been introduced only in the second half of the 16th century.

This arrangement, using a traditional Victorian metal urn, is very classical in its proportion and scale. The old tried-and-trusted rule of making the flower arrangement one and a half times taller than its container works every time if you are trying to create a traditional arrangement.

The flower painters were happy to mix all colours of flowers from all seasons, and we can learn an important lesson in colour theory from their approach. Mixed colours will harmonize if the correct base is used: in the flower arranger's case the base is the greenery, and this will balance the other colours. No single colour should be allowed to predominate in this scheme. The painters' use of a dark background was another clever device for blending the strong flower colours, as well as for creating a moody atmosphere that perfectly suited their masterpieces.

Ingredients

Flowers & foliage
Roses (*Rosa* 'Nicole', 'Blue Moon', 'Stirling Silver', and 'Vicky Brown')
Montbretia (*Crocosmia*)
Delphiniums
Agapanthus
Sweet William (*Dianthus barbatus*)
Anemones
Daffodils (*Narcissus*)
Lilac (*Syringa*)
Stocks (*Matthiola*)
Gloriosa
Lily-of-the-Valley (*Convallaria majalis*)
Eucharis (*Eucharis grandiflora*)
Ranunculus
Tulips (*Tulipa* 'Flaming Parrot')
Crown imperial (*Fritillaria imperialis*)
Larkspur (*Delphinium consolida*)
Peonies (*Paeonia*)
Euphorbia (*Euphorbia fulgens*)
Amaryllis (*Hippeastrum*)
Broom (*Genista*)
Lisianthus (*Eustoma russellianum*)
Achillea (*Achillea* 'Paprika')
Fennel (*Foeniculum vulgare*)
Dill (*Anethum graveolens*)
Hyacinths (*Hyacinthus*)
Jonquil (*Narcissus* 'Jumblie')
Marigolds (*Calendula*)
Forget-me-not (*Myosotis*)
Mimosa (*Acacia*)
Polyanthus (*Primula*)
Silkweed (*Asclepias tuberosa*)
Larch (*Larix*)
Rosemary (*Rosmarinus officinalis*)
Green pussy willow (*Salix caprea*)
Whitebeam (*Sorbus aria* 'Lutescens')
Guelder rose (*Viburnum opulus*)

Other materials
Large metal urn or other large traditional container

Tulipa 'Flaming Parrot'

Trailing arrangement with gerberas

Each day, about 350 different colours and shades of gerbera are sold at the Dutch flower auctions, and popular colours are grown in other flower-producing regions of the world too, notably Israel. These hybrids are now in the top ten of the best-selling flowers in the world. Gerbera stems are leafless but very hairy and can turn mushy and weak if left in deep water for too long. Condition them in deep water but arrange them in not more than 2–3in (5–7.5cm) of water.

Ingredients

Gerberas (*Gerbera*)
'Tamara'
'Barcelona'
'Bordeaux'

Other flowers & foliage
Virginia creeper
(*Vitis quinquefolia*)
Eucalyptus pods
Privet berries (*Ligustrum*)
Trailing ivy (*Hedera helix*)
Guelder rose berries
(*Viburnum opulus*)
Assorted autumn foliage
Hypericum berries
Montbretia seed heads
(*Crocosmia*)
Old man's beard
(*Clematis vitalba*)
Leucospermum (*Leucospermum leutens*)
Love-lies-bleeding (*Amaranthus*)

Other materials
Glass bowl on a stand
2in (5cm) gauge wire mesh

1 Loosely scrunch some wire mesh into a ball to fit snugly into the bowl, then fill it with fresh water, adding some flower food. Gerberas should be conditioned in tepid water mixed with gerbera food. You will need to support the stems to keep them straight.

2 Begin by arranging the foliage, concentrating on the shape you want to achieve in the finished arrangement. A natural-looking arrangement like this requires a variety of foliage, with berries and pods to provide interest and texture. Choose good, trailing foliage to complement the stand, and fuller, bushier foliage for the upright placings. Seed heads add rich colour too – this arrangement uses old man's beard and montbretia seed heads. (You should never gather flowers from the wild, so it is a good idea to grow your own wild plants for arranging.)

3 Next add the *Leucospermum leutens* and the trailing plumes of the love-lies-bleeding to the arrangement.

Finally (right), add the gerberas in groups of three to avoid the arrangement looking patchy and to make it rich, bold, and dramatic.

I have chosen complementary foliage and flowers whose colours make this arrangement particularly suitable for a harvest or Thanksgiving supper. You will need to mist the foliage regularly and make sure that the container is kept topped up with water to prolong the life of the display.

Gerbera 'Tamara'

Rose topiary

A mass of one flower in mixed colours always takes my breath away, and this simple topiary shape never goes out of style. I often take one flower as the inspiration for a design and here the bicolour rose 'Confetti' (or 'Konfetti', as it is sometimes labelled) suggested the colour scheme. I am a big fan of bicolour roses, in which the outer edges of the petals are tipped with another tone, and these two-tone roses are very effective in simple designs such as this. 'Confetti' is grown extensively in South America, as are two similar roses: 'Circus', which is slightly brighter in tone, and 'Ambiance', which usually has a larger head and a slightly more subtle differentiation in its colours.

By choosing shades, tints, and hues either side of the orange and the yellow colours found in the 'Confetti' roses, I have created an analogous harmony in this design. I like to push back the boundaries of accepted colour combinations in flower arranging and so have added another primary colour here. This would not necessarily be considered as a recognized harmony if you were studying colour theory, but colour choice is ultimately very personal.

I love classic topiary, and the round lollipop shape of this design is one of the most often used, being a commonly found form in nature. Fabricated topiary work consists of a basic tree shape, using natural twigs or branches for the stem and then flowers or foliage to create the round ball.

For this rose topiary, birch twigs have been secured around a stronger stem, which has been cemented into a painted ceramic pot. Pushed onto the top of the stems is a small, water-soaked florist's foam ball, which has then been taped in place. Roses have been added to the ball, starting at the top and working down to the base. More foam has been added to the top of the cement base, and eight dahlias have been massed on top of this to hide the mechanics.

Ingredients

Roses (Rosa)
'Confetti'
'Nicole'
'Aalsmeer Gold'

Other flowers & foliage
Dahlias (*Dahlia* 'Arabian Night')
Birch (*Betulus*)

Other materials
Painted flower pot
Small quantity of cement or plaster of Paris
Florist's foam ball
Florist's tape
Florist's wire

Rosa 'Confetti'

Sweet pea and rose posy

This simple posy is natural and loose, with the flowers placed in concentric circles following a style of flower arranging that first became popular in the Victorian period in Britain. From the 1850s a trend began of planting borders with rings of brightly coloured flowers and, as early florists were often head gardeners, it was not long before this style of gardening was paralleled inside the house. Floral displays became less fussy and more controlled, and small bowls would be filled with rings of flowers with the shorter stems being wired into the arrangements. The mechanics for such designs would have been damp sand covered with moss. This trend of displaying flowers in bands soon spread, becoming all the rage in Europe and also in the USA. These early banded flower arrangements were often very stiff and the colours very bright and deep. This soft and natural tied version of a Victorian posy in complementary shades of red and pink mixed with ivory colours, is my contemporary twist on an old idea.

This concentric-circle, hand-tied posy is a little more ambitious than the ordinary mixed-flower, hand-tied bouquet but the technique is almost identical. Begin by cleaning the stems of all your flowers and foliage. Decide which flowers you are going to place next to each other and lay them all out in the order that you plan to use them. You will need to start with a good medium-size central flower. I nearly always choose a rose because it is the perfect shape and size and has a very firm woody stem. Next arrange the sweet peas, placing them into the bouquet at angles, making sure that they are a little bit lower than the central rose. When you have completed the first circle, begin to add the asclepias. Twist the bouquet in your hand and continue to add the love-in-a-mist in another ring. Each layer should be placed slightly lower than the one before to create a dome shape. Add the final three rings of sweet peas, roses, and astilbe, then the galax leaves to edge the posy. Finally, tie it firmly with raffia and trim the ends of all stems to an equal length.

Ingredients

Flowers & foliage
Roses (*Rosa* 'Xtreme')
Sweet peas (*Lathyrus odoratus*)
Love-in-a-mist seed heads
(*Nigella damascena*)
Asclepias (*Asclepias* 'Cinderella')
Astilbe (*Astilbe* 'Montgomery')
Galax leaves (*Galax aphylla*)

Other materials
Raffia to tie

Massed roses with banana leaf twirl

I am fascinated by fresh produce markets, and over the years they have been an enormous source of inspiration to me. I often find myself browsing in the fruit and vegetable markets in London, and on one such visit discovered boxes of banana leaves that had been cut and their spines removed. This made them much more useful than the whole leaves that were available in the flower market. Since then I have been using these beautiful glaucous green leaves in all kind of floral designs. The leaves are subtly fragrant and extremely pliable, which makes them perfect for lining wire baskets or for an unusual, and bio-degradable, wrapping for bouquets. They are also great for decorating dishes of canapés for special occasions and, of course, for steaming food, which is why they are so widely available all over the world now in supermarkets as well as from specialist Asian food stores. Banana leaves are best bought fresh the day you need to use them, as they have a short shelf life. If you do have to store them, keep them in a moist box in a cool, but not chilled, environment. Warm air dries them out too quickly and cold air can turn them yellow and black and makes them too brittle to use.

Commercially grown roses are the perfect flower to practise your hand-tying skills with, as they have very straight and strong woody stems. Most roses have thorns, although there are some new hybrid commercial roses, such as 'Aqua', that have been bred without thorns. A rose without a thorn is a very new development and one that saves a lot of time in the work room of any flower shop, as all roses have to have their thorns removed before they can be presented for sale. On Valentine's Day – when a red rose is still the flower of choice – this means thousands of stems have to be de-thorned. In my workshop we have a commercial machine for removing them, but you still have to check them over by hand before making a hand-tie. I find the easiest way to clean them is to take an ordinary sharp vegetable knife and gently prise off the thorns and the lower leaves, taking care not to damage the skin of the stem.

Ingredients

Roses (*Rosa*)
'Nicole'
'Confetti'
'Tamango'

Other materials
Banana leaves (*Musa*)

Rosa 'Tamango'

Anthuriums in a pumpkin

Anthurium flowers consist of a shiny, waxy bract called a spathe, with a central protruding cylindrical spadix (spike-like cluster of flowers). They bruise easily and, because they look so unusual and have an almost artificial, plastic-like quality, it is common for people to pinch them to see if they are real, which unfortunately leaves a mark. The flowers are also affected by salt, which is carried on the surface of human skin, so try to avoid touching the spathes.

1 Choose a well-balanced pumpkin with a flat base. Slice off the top and cut out a large hole in the flesh. Line the pumpkin with a sheet of thick plastic. Cut a piece of soaked florist's foam to fit in the hole snugly, making sure that it sits higher than the rim.

2 Establish the basic shape of the arrangement with sprigs of oak leaves. The height of the foliage should be at least one and a half times, if not twice that of the container – this is a general rule that applies to most flower arrangements. Add trails of rose hips randomly through the leaves and fill other gaps with hypericum berries.

3 Arrange the branches of chilli peppers (you can buy these as cut flowers) by pushing their stems into the florist's foam. Place the bulrushes throughout the arrangement to add height and arrange the nerines through the foliage to establish the overall shape. The trusses of tomatoes can be wired in place with heavy florist's wire twisted around their stems. Check that all the florist's foam is covered.

Now begin to add the focal flowers – the 'Scarletta' anthuriums (right). These are very dominating so leave plenty of space around each flower and check that all the spadices point outward. Keep the finished arrangement in a cool place and periodically top up the florist's foam with water. If you cannot obtain a suitable pumpkin, you can use another type of squash or a large watermelon.

Ingredients

Flowers & foliage
Oak leaves (*Quercus*)
Rose hips (*Rosa canina*)
Hypericum berries (*Hypericum* 'Autumn Blaze')
Ornamental chilli peppers (*Capsicum*)
Bulrushes (*Typha latifolia*)
Nerines (*Nerine* 'Corusca Major')
Trusses of tomatoes (*Lycopersicum*)
Anthuriums (*Anthurium* 'Scarletta')

Other materials
Large pumpkin (*Curcubita maxima*)
Sheet of thick plastic
Florist's foam
Heavy florist's wire

Autumn cone

This topiary arrangement makes unusual use of seasonal flowers and vegetables. Ornamental cabbages and gourds, both of which are plentiful and inexpensive, have been used with chrysanthemums to create a bright and long-lasting display. As a professional florist I am nearly always working to a set budget, and this often means that I have to use seasonal flowers to make the most of the money available. Vegetables are less expensive than flowers, and so when I am contemplating the components for a large design like this I will often include them to save money. Also, plants are generally less costly than cut flowers. For example, ornamental cabbages are sold both as plants and as cut flowers, but they invariably have much larger heads and are considerably cheaper when purchased as plants. Likewise, artichokes bought on longer stems as cut flowers can cost two or three times as much as their edible relatives. Generally speaking, the longer the stem, the more expensive the flower. When you are creating a topiary form like this, where you will need to cut down the stems in any case, buying fruit and flowers with long stems is an unnecessary expense.

Ingredients

Chrysanthemums
(*Chrysanthemum* Indicum Gr.)
'Shamrock'
'Gompie Geel'
'Purple Pennine Wine'
'Dark Flamenco'

Other flowers & foliage
Ornamental cabbages
(*Brassica oleracea* 'Corgy Pink'
and 'Coblanc')
Ornamental gourds (*Cucurbita maxima*)

Other materials
Base pot
Sturdy birch pole
Cement mix
1in (2.5cm) gauge wire mesh
Moss
Florist's wire

This is a large and heavy topiary design that stands 5ft (1.5m) tall. It therefore needs a very heavy base to ensure that it remains stable. Most often I will use concrete for my topiary bases because it is heavy and inexpensive. First, place a sturdy birch pole into the centre of the base pot and cement it into place. Next create a cone-shaped cage of 1in (2.5cm) gauge wire mesh filled with moss, and attach it with wire around the central pole. Once the structure is secure, you are ready to add the vegetables and flowers. Begin with the heavy round heads of the ornamental cabbages, placing them at different heights across the cone shape. These are the largest and widest items of plant material used here, and you will need to arrange the chrysanthemums and gourds in groups of three to create the same proportions. Only the large-headed, vibrantly coloured standard 'Shamrock' chrysanthemums are visually strong enough to be used as single stems.

Chrysanthemum (Indicum Gr.)
'Shamrock'

Hanging delphinium ball

Hanging decorations are good when you have a vast space to fill or very little room for floor-standing arrangements, and should be created on site to achieve the best shape. This kind of display looks spectacular with delphiniums. About fifty varieties are sold as cut flowers, but sadly the full range of colours has a very limited season. Buy ones that have been post-harvest treated in a solution of silver nitrate – which makes them stronger – and condition them well before using them.

Ingredients

Flowers & foliage
Cotinus (*Cotinus coggygria* 'Royal Purple')
Privet (*Ligustrum*)
Cotoneaster
Rose hips (*Rosa canina*)
Delphiniums (*Delphinium* 'White Arrow' and 'Yvonne')
Hydrangeas (*Hydrangea macrophylla* 'Blue Tit')
Roses (*Rosa* 'Yellow Success')

Other materials
Box of florist's foam
Large bucket
Two semi-spherical hanging baskets
Florist's wire
Strong rope
Wire mesh

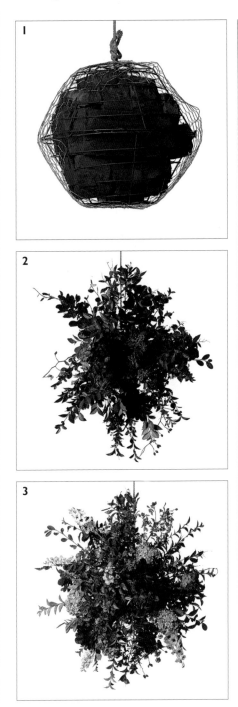

1 Thoroughly soak a box of florist's foam in a large bucket of water, then shape the foam blocks into circles and place them in the hanging baskets. Wire the baskets together to make a ball, then knot the rope securely to the top. Cover the whole ball with wire mesh to keep the two halves together and the florist's foam intact, and to increase the strength of the ball. At this stage you can place the ball in water for a further soaking if you wish.

2 Establish a round shape with the foliage, making sure that you have covered the florist's foam. I have used cotinus, privet, cotoneaster, and rose hips (*Rosa canina*). You will need to hang the ball at a comfortable height for working, ideally in its final position. Make sure that the girders from which you are hanging it are strong enough – it will be extremely heavy when full of water and plant material. If hanging one in a marquee, ask the supplier to provide a suitable construction.

3 Add enough delphiniums to establish the outline, then insert the hydrangeas. Add most of the delphiniums at the final stage, as they are quite fragile. Hold them at their bases to prevent them snapping when you insert them into the foam. Check the shape from all sides and from a distance.

Finally (right), add the roses, mist well, and raise the ball into position. Keep a plastic sheet under the ball for several hours to catch the water drips.

Mothers' Day nosegay

Mothers' Day, which falls on the fourth Sunday in Lent in the UK and on the second Sunday in May in most of the rest of the world, is a day for spoiling mothers, and is one of the busiest days in the florist's calendar. Interestingly enough, the tradition in Britain started when many young people lived "in service" in large houses and estates and were given one Sunday to return home and visit their mothers. In England a tradition was born of taking wild flowers, most notably violets plucked from the hedgerows and abundant at that time of year, home with them as a gift. However, the origins of a special time for showing appreciation of our mothers actually go back to ancient Greece: as part of a three-day festival to honour Cybele, the mother of the gods, flowers were collected and offered to her.

I love Mothers' Day because the young visitors to my shop are so instinctively drawn to the scents and colours. They are encouraged to make their own choices of flowers and the colour of the bow, and so enter into the creative experience of buying flowers.

Ingredients

Flowers & foliage
Forget-me-nots (*Myosotis*)
Sweet peas (*Lathyrus odoratus*)
Grape hyacinths (*Muscari*)
Tulips (*Tulipa* 'Fancy Frill')
Narcissus
(*Narcissus* 'Bridal Crown')
Galax leaves (*Galax aphlla*)

Other materials
Raffia

Narcissus 'Paper White'

1 Although traditional 19th-century nosegays were wired, this simpler version is unwired. Choose flowers with different textures and colours so that the rings that make up the nosegay are distinct. The idea of a nosegay is that it is scented, so select fragrant flowers.

First condition your cut flowers by snipping their stems and leaving them in nutrient-enriched water for several hours. Strip the leaves off all the stems, but make sure that you remove only the lower leaves from the forget-me-nots and tulips, or the stems will be too weak.

2 Take a tulip as your middle or focal flower and surround it with a ring of forget-me-nots, then a ring of narcissus and one of grape hyacinths, to build up concentric circles.

5 To finish the Mothers' Day nosegay, make a bow with a length of wide ribbon of a contrasting colour (see Techniques, pages 180–1) and tie it over the raffia. Finally, trim all the ends of the stems in the nosegay so that it is comfortable to hold in the hand.

Stephanotis floribunda

3 As you add each ring, bind the stems together gently with raffia. You can make the nosegay in your hand if this feels comfortable. However, if it feels awkward, use a vase or a glass to hold the flowers as you work. The next layer in this arrangement is a ring of tulips. As before, tie the stems into the nosegay with raffia.

4 The outer ring of flowers is made of sweet peas. When you have bound the sweet pea stems with raffia, edge the whole bunch with galax leaves. These frame the flowers nicely and also help protect the flower heads. Bind the stems of the galax leaves with more raffia.

Nosegay alternatives

There are many different flowers you can select to make a scented posy. Try the following:

Central flower:

- Tulip

- Rose

- Anemone

Small fragrant varieties:

- Primroses (*Primula vulgaris*)

- Sweet violets (*Viola odorata*)

- Wax flowers (*Stephanotis floribunda*)

- Lily-of-the-valley (*Convallaria majalis*)

- Periwinkles (*Vinca major*)

- Bluebells (*Hyacinthoides campanulatus*)

- Cornflowers (*Centaurea cyanus*)

- Stars of Bethlehem or chincherinchees (*Ornithogalum thyrsoides*)

- Everlasting peas (*Lathyrus latifolius*)

- Freesias

Aromatic flowering herbs:

- Tansy (*Tanacetum vulgare*)

- Rosemary (*Rosmarinus officinalis*)

- Lavender (*Lavandula*)

- Dill (*Anethum graveolens*)

- Sage (*Salvia*)

Contemporary

Submerged phalaenopsis orchids

This arrangement was originally designed for a wedding reception, but I have created variations of it for contract work. Unfortunately, phalaenopsis orchids begin to go papery after about five days. Although cymbidiums fare rather better, the water will start to become cloudy after about five days and will need changing. The most spectacularly long-lasting orchids are the vandas, which can continue to look good for more than two weeks.

Ingredients

Flowers & foliage
20–25 phalaenopsis orchids
(*Phalaenopsis*)

Other materials
Cylindrical glass vase
Roll of aluminium florist's wire

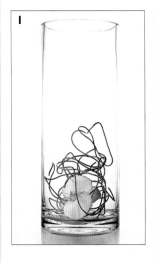

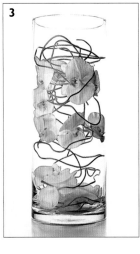

1 Place the head of a phalaenopsis orchid in the bottom of an empty, clean glass cylinder vase. Lightly scrunch up some aluminium wire and place it in the bottom third of the vase.

2 Add further phalaenopsis heads and more wire, positioning the flower heads carefully to avoid damaging them and distributing them evenly. It is very important that you use enough wire to prevent the orchid heads floating to the surface when you add the water.

3 Carry on adding flower heads and wire until you reach the top of the vase, then top it up with water. (If you add the water earlier you will find it difficult to keep the flower heads submerged: without enough wire to hold them down they have a tendency to float to the top.)

Calla lily and orchid ring

Although this arrangement is very contemporary, its structure is a ring, which is a traditional form in floral design. Throughout the world in every culture, circles and rings have been steeped in symbolism, and so were among the earliest and most used forms for the arrangement of plant material. The colour combination used here is harmonious and suits the simplicity of its shape. (When an association of colours is made up of two or three colours that are similar, it is known as an analogous colour combination.) The choice of plant material for this kind of design is crucial to its success: because the stems and flower heads will be in contact with the water, they need to be strong and waxy. Calla lilies are excellent because they are tough, long-lasting, and have very supple stems, which are perfect for this type of arrangement. Orchids are also quite flexible and very durable and combine effectively with the lilies here.

Take each stem of calla lily and gently rub it with your thumb and forefinger to make it more supple. When all the stems are relaxed, arrange them around the inside of the glass bowl. Next, simply twist the dendrobiums around the calla lilies to give the arrangement movement. Take care to ensure that the stems lie in the base of the bowl and that you stretch the orchids to the maximum without breaking or damaging any stems. The arrangement should look natural, although it is actually quite confined in the bowl, so use the orchids to bind around the central calla lilies as a vine winds around a branch. When you have completed the design, top up the bowl with water until all the stems are beneath the water line.

Ingredients

Flowers & foliage
Calla lilies (*Zantedeschia aethiopica* 'Florex Gold')
Orchids (*Dendrobium* 'Tang')

Other materials
Wide glass bowl

Sunflower roses

I had been attaching foliage, reeds, twigs, and flowers to the outside of containers for a long time before it suddenly became chic to place such plant material on the inside of the glass. Customizing a container in this way means that the material lasts longer, so this type of display is appropriate for corporate work. I have been on a journey of discovery of what works, how long it lasts, and how effective it is: these croton leaves are one of my favourite versions of this design.

Ingredients

Flowers & foliage
Bunch of croton leaves
(*Codiaeum variegatum*)
Bunch of montbretia berries
(*Crocosmia aurea* 'Emily McKenzie')
10 mini sunflowers (*Helianthus*)
6 roses (*Rosa* 'Sphinx')
Bunch of ivy trails (*Hedera*)
3 autumn hydrangeas
(*Hydrangea macrophylla*)

Other materials
Block of florist's foam
Glass column vase
Stub wires

1 Place a block of florist's foam in the centre of a glass column vase. The block should be about 2in (5cm) taller than the glass vase and should not fit too snugly inside it. Fill the gap between the foam and the glass with croton leaves, cutting off the stalks so that they sit neatly on the bottom of the vase. Croton leaves have quite varied markings, so alternate the colours to create visual impact.

2 Montbretia berries have lovely curved stems and so suit being arranged in a ring around the top of a vase. Cut individual stems of berries from the main stalk and place them into the foam so that they create a wreath of berries around the foam. Place the berries in the same direction but at different heights to give more texture and density. Continue until you have hidden the foam and have a lovely dense ring of berries.

3 Place the miniature sunflowers around the inside of the wreath, leaving the centre free. Make sure the stalks are pushed well into the foam, as sunflowers are thirsty drinkers and will need to be able to soak up a lot of moisture from the foam. Next (right), add the roses, creating a group in the centre of the display. Weave trails of ivy around the roses to give movement to the design and cover exposed foam, using stub wires to hold them in place.

Star fruit and crown imperials

Crown imperials have a very short spring season. Some people find their musty smell a little off-putting, but you can overcome this by placing a few drops of bleach with their flower food and changing their water daily. Their curvy stems and radiant petals in either bright yellow or orange make them a great favourite of mine. There is a touching legend attached to these flowers, which explains their unusual stance and the fact that they shed water from their petals: when Jesus was taken from the Garden of Gethsemane to his crucifixion, the crown imperial is said to have bowed its head in remorse and its petals filled with tears. The petals continue to produce water even when they are displayed as cut flowers. The crown imperial's tiny relatives, Fritillaria meleagris, *also have bowed heads and wonderful markings.*

Ingredients

Flowers & foliage
Craspedia (*Craspedia globosa*)
Crown imperials
(*Fritillaria imperialis*)
Bear grass (*Dasylirion*)
Bun moss (*Leucobryum glaucum*)

Other materials
Star fruit (*Averrhoa carambola*)
Round glass bowl
Glass cylinder of the same height
Small stones or pebbles

1 The first step is to condition the crown imperials. Cut the base of each stem on an angle so that the flowers can drink easily. Then place the stems in a bucket of nutrient-enriched water for several hours. In the meantime, prepare the rest of the material for the arrangement. Take a yellow star fruit – not too ripe or it will be too soft to cut cleanly and will rot quickly. Cut across the width of the fruit with a sharp knife so that the pieces are star-shaped. Take the yellow craspedias and remove the flower heads or "balls" from the stems.

I have used a glass fish bowl for this arrangement, but you can choose an alternative container, providing it is transparent, as the idea is to make a feature of the container as well as of the flowers themselves. Start to line the inside of the fish bowl with bun moss. Make a pattern so that the slices of star fruit and craspedia heads are surrounded by moss,

2 Continue to line the sides of the bowl with moss, adding the slices of star fruit and craspedia heads at intervals. Because the container is curved, you will have to use a padding of moss inside the bowl to prevent the "lining" from slipping. Leave a space in the middle in which to stand a flat-based glass cylinder. Continue to build up the lining of moss, slices of star fruit, and craspedia heads until you have covered the whole of the inside of the bowl. Before you reach the rim, place the glass cylinder inside the bowl, making sure that the rims of both vessels are almost level.

Fill in the space between the inner cylinder and the outer bowl using more moss and some small stones or pebbles for extra bulk. Make sure that the stones are hidden and that the craspedia heads and slices of star fruit are evenly distributed around the bowl. Then fill the inner glass cylinder with water.

Variations on the theme

You can create all sorts of variations on this theme, taking, for example, any variety of red or orange lilies and arranging them in the same way. You can decorate a glass container by matching the colours of the cut flowers with fruits, for example:

- Cherries (*Prunus avium*)

- Ornamental hot or chilli peppers (*Capsicum frutescens*)

- Hard red berries such as barberries (*Berberis*)

- Sea buckthorn (*Hippophäe rhamnoides*)

- Cranberries (*Vaccinium*)

- Pitangas or Surinam cherries (*Eugenia uniflora*)

- The small orange fruits of Chinese lanterns or Cape gooseberries (*Physalis*)

- Knobbly red lychees (*Litchi chinensis*).

3 Take some long strands of bear grass and tie them together at one end, fixing this knotted end to a hook or door knob so that you have both hands free to make a plait. Take care not to cut your hands on the grass as the blades are sharp. Then fix the plait of grass around the rim of the bowl and knot the two ends together securely and discreetly at the back.

Once your container is prepared, take the crown imperials and strip away any leaves lower down on the stems. (This is because leaves in the water will make the water turn green and encourage the growth of bacteria. Apart form being unsightly, this will also also reduce the longevity of the flowers.) Make sure that you leave the foliage on the upper stems as it will add to the overall effect. The stems of the crown imperials will curve naturally toward the light, which will give shape and movement to the arrangement.

4 The success of this arrangement depends on its one-colour theme, which is all the more strikingly simple because only one type of flower has been used. The base of the arrangement complements and enhances the majesty of the crown imperials.

Crown imperials have a very strong shape, which makes them quite awkward to arrange with other flowers. Also, like tulips, they tend to move with the light and so have a mind of their own about where they will eventually end up in your arrangement. This collection, arranged in a glass cylinder of water concealed by the moss and star fruit, has twisted and moved into new directions of its own. Nature is a great teacher, and I am sure they have acquired a more interesting shape than any arrangement I might have achieved.

Snake grass vase filled with heliconias

The best floral arrangements use containers that complement the flowers and lend a sculptural feel to the whole design. Customizing containers for floral arrangements has become one of my trademarks, and a simple and effective way to do it is to use double-sided sticky tape to attach leaves or other plant material to a vase. Snake grass is an excellent reed to use because it lasts well and has a lovely texture that sets off most flowers, particularly tropical varieties.

Ingredients

Flowers & foliage
Bundle of snake grass (*Scirpus tabernaemontani* 'Zebrinus')
Dogwood twigs (*Cornus*)
Heliconias (*Heliconia bihai* 'Emerald Forest')
Yucca leaves (*Yucca aloifolia*)
New Zealand flax leaves (*Phormium*)

Other materials
Cylindrical glass vase
Double-sided sticky tape
Bundle of raffia

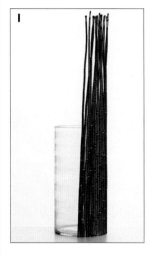

1 Apply strips of double-sided sticky tape to the outer surface of the glass vase, from top to bottom and completely covering it. Stick the strands of snake grass to the vase one at a time, working from bottom to top. Be selective when choosing the snake grass, using the straightest stems. Continue adding the strips of snake grass until you have covered the whole vase.

2 Cut the raffia into 12 lengths or more, each at least double the circumference of the vase. Tie all the raffia lengths around the vase and knot them tightly together, then trim the ends. The snake grass will dry out and the vase will last indefinitely, though its colour will fade over time.

Other reeds, such as mikado grass, would give the same effect as snake grass. Or you could use yucca tips.

3 Carefully trim the top of the snake grass so that it is straight all the way around and flush with the top of the vase. Fill the vase with tepid water, then add some flower food.

Arrange the dogwood twigs in the vase first, as they will help to anchor the large heliconias (see opposite). Trim the heliconias to length and arrange them in the vase. Finally, add the yucca and flax leaves, which will give extra colour and interest to the arrangement.

Red Perspex tray

Perspex is currently much in fashion, and it is a very useful material because you can have boxes, trays, or other containers made to any specification. This gives the florist a lot of flexibility in designing arrangements for parties, weddings, or contract work. I love clear Perspex, but there are also some wonderfully rich colours that can be used to make original containers or pedestals. It is relatively inexpensive and lasts quite well if you take care not to scratch the surface.

1 This box has been designed as a 12in (30cm) square, 2in (5cm) deep table centrepiece. It is made from ½in (1cm) thick Perspex, which makes it very sturdy, and the bright red colour works well with vibrant flowers.

Fill the box with soaked florist's foam to the height of the edge of the container. To conceal the foam I have tucked some coloured reeds between the foam and the Perspex.

2 Tie the remainder of the reeds into four equal bundles, using raffia. Mark the foam into nine equal squares. Start by placing the nerines in one corner square, add the yellow roses next to them, then insert the delphinium florets. Make sure that each group of flowers forms a neat square and that they are all the same height. Tuck a bundle of the canes under this first row of flowers and over the edge of the Perspex. Beside the delphiniums add the red roses, then continue to create the second and third rows of flowers as shown and listed opposite. Finally, tie together the bunches of reeds where they meet at the corners, using coloured raffia.

Ingredients

Flowers & foliage
9 nerines (*Nerine bowdenii* 'Corusca Major')
9 yellow roses (*Rosa* 'Tressor 2000')
1 stem blue hybrid delphinium (*Delphinium elatum* 'Alie Duyvensteyn')
9 cherry roses (*Rosa* 'Cherry Lady')
1 stem purple hybrid delphinium (*Delphinium elatum* 'Harlecijn')
1 sunflower (*Helianthus annuus* 'Teddy Bear')
4 lilac roses (*Rosa* 'Coolwater')
1 chrysanthemum (*Chrysanthemum* Indicum Gr. 'Shamrock')
3 tangerine Singapore orchids (*Aacocentrum curvifolium* 'Tang')

Other materials
Red square Perspex box or tray (approx. 12in/30cm square x 2in/5cm deep)
2 blocks of florist's foam
Large bunch of brightly coloured reeds (at least 14in/35cm long)
Brightly coloured raffia

Rose petal cube

This is such a simple idea and yet so romantic. I am convinced that a few glass cube vases are essential to any flower arranger's container collection, and it is an especially good idea to have several of different sizes that will fit inside one another. Alternatively, you could use containers of varying shapes but of a similar depth, as I have done in this design. The petals will last only for a few days, so I recommend you prepare an arrangement like this as late as you can.

Place the tumbler in the centre of the glass vase and fill it with water mixed with flower food. Strip all the flowers and foliage of their lower branches and leaves and place them in neat piles. Using a sharp knife, make long downward movements along the length of the rose stems to prise off the thorns without damaging the skin.

To begin making the hand-tie, take one central rose in your left hand (if you are right-handed) and then place another piece of plant material at an angle just to the left of it. Add three more stems, then, using both hands, twist the bunch around a quarter of a turn. Add another five stems and turn the bunch again. Repeat this at least eight times until you have used all the plant material. Now tie the bunch with some wired florist's tie and trim the stems. Place the freshly plucked petals between the tumbler and the glass cube vase, then place the hand-tie in the tumbler.

Ingredients

Flowers & foliage
10 'Pretty Woman' roses
10 'Tressor 2000' roses
7 stems of dill
(*Anethum graveolens*)
5 stems of gloriosa
(*Gloriosa rothschildiana*)
Bunch of ivy berries
(*Hedera helix*)
10 stems of lady's mantle
(*Alchemilla mollis*)

Other materials
Glass tumbler
6in (15cm) glass cube vase
Selection of rose petals
Wired florist's tie

Roses and feathers

Feathers can make great accessories to use with flowers; I love this marabou-feather trim, and it is available in a variety of colours. Here, used with a frosted vase, it has an almost fur-like appearance and makes this simple vase arrangement look very festive. You can buy feather trims and feathers from some floral sundries wholesalers, and they are also easy to find in trimming shops all over the world. I use them a lot in wedding work, both to edge bouquets and in arrangements.

Ingredients

Flowers & foliage
16 roses (*Rosa* 'Ruby Red')

Other materials
Frosted glass cube vase
Clear sticky tape
Length of white marabou
feathers

1 When you want to create a geometric shape without any visible mechanics, simple and inexpensive sticky tape can provide the answer. Here, a lovely frosted glass vase is given a simple grid of tape to hold the flowers in a square shape, while the vase loses none of its beautiful translucency. Simply cut six lengths of sticky tape and place three across the vase in one direction, adding the other three across these at right angles to create 16 equal-size holes in the top of the vase, as shown above.

The same technique can work just as effectively with a shallow crystal bowl. You could also use floral tape, which is stronger and more waterproof than ordinary sticky tape. Although not transparent, it will usually be kept out of sight; alternatively, a white variety is available.

2 Once the tape grid is in place, all you need to do is place a rose in each of the 16 holes in the grid. With the addition of the marabou-feather trim, this simple arrangement is transformed into a "million-dollar" look for a fraction of that price. If they get wet, marabou feathers smell a little "earthy", so try to secure them above the water line. (Of course, if they do get wet, they will dry out and fluff up really quickly.)

Feathers add a lovely soft movement to flower arrangements, and there are all sorts of variations you can try on this theme. Pale pink and lilac roses work really well with dyed feather boas, while a bowl of cream hyacinths looks fabulous with a matching feather trim. Or for an even more opulent feel – perhaps for a wedding – why not try using ostrich feathers?

Rubber vase display

The choice of container is fundamental to any floral design, and one as dominant as this is going to play a particularly crucial role in the choice of plant material. The container has the primary function of providing water – the lifeblood of the natural world – but it will also dictate the overall size and final appearance of your design. I love to make my own containers so that they become an integral part of my arrangements; I also like to use ones that create a visual link with the flowers. In choosing a suitable vessel you will need to think about its colour, texture, style, size, and shape, and to ensure that it harmonizes with the blooms. Where it is as colourful and bold as the one shown here, it is important that the flowers should not try to compete for attention, but rather harmonize with it. For this multicoloured rubber vase I chose bold flowers linked together by many different types of foliage. The deep black berries of Viburnum tinus *and the velvety grey foliage of* Senecio greyii *help to tone down the luminosity, while the lime-green sprigs of* Alchemilla mollis *add to the brightness of the flowers. It is the balance of foliage and flowers that make this design work.*

This round posy has been constructed as a hand-tied bouquet and then placed into the container. Choose a selection of blooms that will fit the size and height of your container and lay them all out in front of you in groups. Remove all lower foliage from the stems below the approximate binding point. Select your central flower and hold it at the binding point between the thumb and forefinger of your left hand, if you are right-handed. (Usually one binds into the weaker hand, leaving the stronger hand to pass material and use the scissors when the design is complete.) Take the next flower and place it at right angles to the central one. After you have added five pieces of plant material, use both hands to twist the material in your left hand about a quarter of a turn so that you are now working on another side of the bunch. Continue adding and twisting until the the bouquet is completed. Trim the ends of the stems and place the posy in the vase.

Ingredients

Dahlias
Dahlia 'Charlie Kenwood'
Dahlia 'Arabian Nights'
Dahlia 'Molly Mooney'
Dahlia 'Piper's Pink'
Dahlia 'Karma Fuchsiana'

Other flowers & foliage
Bunch of senecio
(Senecio greyii)
Lady's mantle (Alchemilla mollis)
Viburnum berries
(Viburnum tinus)
Rose hips (Rosa canina)
Cotinus (Cotinus coggygria)
Orange roses (Rosa 'Naranga')
Pink roses (Rosa 'Milano')
Tansies (Tanacetum vulgare)

Other materials
Tall straight-sided vase

Dahlia 'Ruskin Dance'

Pillar of carnations and chrysanthemums

I cannot say how many times in my career as a florist I have heard people, when they are ordering flowers or describing their dislikes, name carnations and chrysanthemums as their least favourite flowers. I cannot abide flower snobbery and don't like to defame any variety – for me they all have some intrinsic beauty or use. There is a belief among florists that a great floral designer can create something beautiful even from material found in the flower shop waste bin. And in most cases this is true – a winning arrangement does not always require the most exotic or expensive blooms. One of the features I admire about carnations and chrysanthemums is that, being multi-petalled flowers, they have great textures. I also adore the intensity and diversity of colours that these much-maligned flowers have produced for their breeders over the years. They are also relatively inexpensive, which means you can create a large and striking arrangement without huge cost. And one more positive characteristic – such a display will last for ages because both these flowers have tremendous stamina.

Although this colourful display was completely dictated by the choice of flowers, the photographer, Kevin Summers, felt sure that the inspiration had really come from Marge's hat in the famous TV cartoon *The Simpsons*!

To create this arrangement you need to use the large blocks of florist's foam that you can buy commercially. Fit them snugly into the urn and build them up into a rectangular shape by adding other blocks onto the base and skewering them together with a small bamboo cane. Secure the structure with reel wire and, when you are sure that your mechanics are dependable, begin to add the foliage. I used some dark green ivy leaves to cover the foam before adding flowers in blocks of colours, mixing them and using both chrysanthemums and carnations randomly to maximum effect. You will need about 200 flower heads for this design.

Ingredients

Flowers & foliage
Chrysanthemums (various colours)
Standard carnations (*Dianthus*) (various varieties, including some fancy bicolours and the fashionable lime-green 'Prado')
Ivy berries (*Hedera helix*)

Other materials
Urn
Blocks of florist's foam
Small bamboo cane
Reel wire

Dianthus 'Prado'

Wild roses

Garden roses are among my favourite flowers, and to my mind one of the most sensuous floral combinations can be created by mixing these exquisite fragrant flowers with wild ivy. To create a natural arrangement you need to consider its movement and rhythm – qualities that are all around us in the natural world. When you gaze at the dancing branches of blossom in the spring or the gentle swaying of a wheat field in midsummer you are witnessing the rhythm and movement of nature. A great flower arrangement will effectively simulate these natural rhythms, giving it something extra – a quality that excites and pleases. By contrast, a display that lacks "movement" will appear solid, fragmented, and ordinary. For some designers, an understanding of rhythm is almost instinctual, marking them out as "natural" flower designers; for others the development of a feeling of rhythm comes with experience and practice. In this arrangement, the perceived movement is achieved through the progression of colour and the use of the ivy to move the eye across the design and give it continuity: the trailing ivy provides a strong visual line along which the eye is drawn and stimulated.

To create this hand-tied design you need to remove the lower foliage and thorns from the roses and clean the branches of ivy to create some bare stems that are easy to handle. Start by taking one rose and a branch of ivy, holding them lightly in one hand between your thumb and forefinger. (I am right-handed so I hold them in my left hand so that I can use my right to add further stems.) Continue to add flowers and foliage at an angle to the left of the original stems. After adding about five stems, twist the bunch in your hand and continue to do so every five or seven stems so that you are working on all sides of the bunch. When you have completed it, add some ivy trails around the edge and work them through and across the posy so that the cut ends are able to drink water. Tie the bunch with ivy, wind some more ivy around the stems, then place it into a cube glass vase so that the stems are concealed and the design is encircled by ivy.

Ingredients

Flowers & foliage
A selection of garden roses
5 branches of ivy (*Hedera helix*)
with berries
7 stems of trailing ivy

Other materials
6in (15cm) glass cube vase

East meets South

This symmetrical vase arrangement is a perfect example of how well flowers from hot climates but different habitats can work together. Here I have mixed orchids from Asia with native African proteas. Both are very strong and long-lasting and are perfect flowers for corporate or regular contract work where reliability is paramount.

The African and Asian continents are very important sources of cut flowers because they have unusual and rich native flora. Thanks to their favourable climate, expertise, and less expensive labour, African and Asian growers can produce flowers that it would be impossible to grow either in Europe or in America (except in the most southern parts), because these plants require so much warmth, light, and intensive care. The cultivation period of orchids is traditionally long, and until recently this made them relatively expensive flowers to produce. "In vitro" cultivation of orchids has now become much more common and has resulted in a plentiful and affordable supply, although these "cloned" orchids do not last as long as conventionally grown ones.

To create this arrangement, wrap a glass column vase in banana leaves, using double-sided tape. Fill it with water mixed with flower food.

To create a symmetrical design, the expanse of flowers should be of identical width, height, and depth. To begin this design with a good and sound structure, arrange a few branches of contorted hazel in the vase first. This acts as the mechanics for the arrangement and is an excellent device when you are using a clear glass vase. Next add some snake grass for height, the proteas to fill the arrangement, and a few branches of fatsia foliage around the edge of the vase to soften the sides. Make sure that all the stems radiate from the centre of the vase. Use the three colours and varieties of the linear spikes of orchids to create the radial from the centre and take the eye to the edge of the display. Finally, use some small branching proteas to fill any gaps in the arrangement.

Ingredients

Proteas
Leucadendron 'Safari Sunset'
Leucadendron discolor
Leucadendron laureolum

Orchids
Mokkara 'Tangerine Tang'
Arachnis 'Maggie Oei'
Aranthera 'James Storei'

Other flowers & foliage
Banana leaves (*Musa ornata*)
Contorted hazel
(*Corylus avellana* 'Contorta')
Snake grass
(*Equisetum giganteum*)
Fatsia leaves and seed heads
(*Fatsia japonica*)

Other materials
Cylindrical glass vase
Double-sided tape

Horse-chestnut wreath

In the part of East Anglia, England, where I was born, there are still many fine horse-chestnut trees, and they have a special place in my memories. I have always loved the beginning of spring, when these majestic trees look so graceful with all their pink and cream blossom. And toward the end of the summer, when the plentiful crop of chestnuts that will ensure the trees' survival appears, it is hard not to be enticed and inspired by their glossy brown and tactile coats.

Ingredients

Flowers & foliage
Sphagnum moss
(*Sphagnum auriculatum*)
Spanish moss
(*Tillandsia usneoides*)
Horse-chestnuts
(*Aesculus hippocastanum*)
Old man's beard (*Clematis vitalba* 'Emerald Forest')

Other materials
Wire wreath frame
0.56mm blue annealed reel wire
Hot glue gun

1 To make a wreath in the traditional method you will need a bag of sphagnum moss. This is usually sold through foliage wholesalers or garden centres and is relatively inexpensive. Tease the moss out to get some air into it, and remove any bits of bark, wood, grass, leaves, and insects.

Take the end of the reel wire and secure it onto the frame. Then, adding the moss in pieces, wrap it around the frame, binding it in place with the reel wire. Continue binding the moss onto the ring all the way around. Trim off any excess pieces of moss so that the finished moss ring looks neat.

Now is a good time to switch on your glue gun. Glue guns are available as "hot-melt" and "low-melt", and it is worth investing in both types: low-melt glue guns will not score natural material and are great for sticking leaves and reeds. Heavier material, such as branches and nuts, benefit from hotter glue, which is stronger.

2 Next, take a few handfuls of Spanish moss and bind the pieces around the top of the frame in the same way, to give the ring a lovely grey effect.

You are now ready to begin sticking the chestnuts in place. I find that it is easier to get a good round shape if you work around the wreath frame in circles. Try to choose chestnuts of a similar size, and grade them before you begin to work. Start by sticking a circle of chestnuts around the top of the wreath and work all the way around to complete the circle before beginning the next one. Continue in this way, working from the centre of the wreath outward to its edge, then from the centre inward. Add small pieces of old man's beard between and around the horse-chestnuts.

Finally, fill in any gaps in the wreath with a few more pieces of moss to make it look natural. Watch out for any drops of glue that may be visible and cover them with moss.

Apple vases

Although this is a very contemporary use of fruit with flowers, the idea of using fruit to enhance flowers has been explored by many different artists over the centuries; indeed, a visit to an art gallery is sure to be a great inspiration to any floral designer. These two arrangements are both inspired by nature and use very similar flowers, but they are in different styles.

The arrangement on the left is a linear one, in which the focus is on creating an interesting form using lines. Such designs often evolve from seeing flowers growing in their natural habitat, and the material used is generally limited so that the lines remain strong. Bold colours, or combinations of colours, help to enrich the linear arrangement; here brightly coloured heliconias have been used on their own. The arrangement on the right is a more traditional massed one, in which the heliconias have been mixed with crab apples. The stems all radiate from the centre of the display, in one of the most used and popular decorative patterns in floral designs. It is also one that takes its inspiration from the architecture of plant forms – many plants, trees, and even flowers themselves follow this pleasing pattern.

To create the linear design on the left of the picture, skewer small apples together on several lengths of bamboo cane, each the height of the vase. Place them around the inside edge of the vase, adding some green stems of heliconias between each line of apples. Fill the centre of the vase with blocks of florist's foam, then add the heliconias to the foam in a linear upright arrangement. Finally, wire more apples on the top of the vase to hide the foam.

To create the arrangement on the right, half-fill the glass vase with apples and water, then begin to create the radial of stems by arranging the heliconias and stems of crab apples. When you have a good all-round shape with the material radiating from the centre, add more apples around the stems, filling the vase to the top so that all the stems are hidden. To complete the arrangement, add a little vine around the top of the vase to lead the eye from the base to the flowers.

Ingredients

Flowers & foliage
Cider apples
(*Malus domestica* 'Crimson King')
Heliconia
(*Heliconia psittacorum* 'Parrot')
Clematis vine (*Clematis vitalba*)
Crab apples
(*Malus* 'Red Sentinel')

Other materials
Bamboo canes
Two cylindrical glass vases
Florist's foam blocks
Florist's wire

Christmas red and green

This simple glass cube has to be one of the most versatile vases, and is one of my favourite. There are just so many ways you can dress a vase like this, making it a store-cupboard essential for any flower arranger. Stones, sand, and gravel all work well placed between the glass and the foam to provide different looks. Fruit, nuts, and spices have also featured in my glass cube arrangements. Here, I have used natural dogwood in three colours to create a striped effect.

Ingredients

Dogwood twigs
Black (*Cornus alba* 'Siberica')
Red (*Cornus alba* 'Argenteo-Marginata')
Green (*Cornus alba* 'Aurea')

Other flowers & foliage
Viburnum (*Viburnum tinus*)
Green balls (*Asclepias physocarpa* 'Moby Dick')
Chrysanthemums (*Chrysanthemum* Indicum Gr. 'Dracula')
Carnations (*Dianthus* 'America')

Other materials
Glass cube vase
Blocks of florist's foam
Decorative reel wire

1 Soak florist's foam blocks and fit them into the glass cube vase, wiring them together if necessary to keep them secure. Leave enough space around the edges to insert at least one row of dogwood twigs between the glass and the foam on each side. Cut the stems of dogwood to the height of the inside of the vase and arrange them in stripes of different colours. I have chosen flowers in the same red and green spectrum, some with both colours in a single flower.

2 First add the foliage to establish the shape of the arrangement. I have used viburnum and the lime-green balls of asclepias. For an arrangement like this it is important that the colours are really emphasized, and the best way to do this is to group the flowers and foliage. In European floristry, decorative reel wire is often used to wire together flower heads, berries, and even twigs. In this design, I have used copper wire to join together lengths of dogwood twigs to form a decorative garland. You can use the offcuts for this, making a design feature from what would otherwise end up in the waste bucket. Add groups of the two varieties of chrysanthemums to the arrangement, then weave the twig garland over the top of the design as shown on the right.

Nerine living topiary

Nerines are very graceful flowers with a thin stem that bears an umbel of between six and ten flowers. Agapanthus are similar and also work very well in this kind of design, where a number of flowers are massed together and tied at the base of the heads to create a living topiary. This very simple and elegant design suits most occasions and situations. It is perfect for a table centrepiece, having some height but still allowing guests to see across the table and enjoy the company.

Ingredients

Flowers & foliage
25 nerines (*Nerine bowdenii* 'Lady Cynthia')
7 bright pink carnations (*Dianthus* 'Farida')
7 lime-green carnations (*Dianthus* 'Prado Refit')
1 cymbidium orchid stem (*Cymbidium* 'Green Fantasy')

Other materials
Wired florist's tie
Roll of aluminium wire
Florist's fix
3in (8cm) pin holder
Glass dish

Nerines are available as cut flowers all year round. In their natural habitat, these bulb flowers sparkle in the autumn. Originally from South Africa, where they grow on mountain slopes, these exotic flowers have become naturalized on the Channel Island of Guernsey. (According to legend, some bulbs were cast ashore from a ship travelling from Japan to Britain via South Africa.) By 1920, nerines were available at the Covent Garden Flower Market in London, and they have since gone on to become one of the "all year round" flowers championed by the huge flower relay organizations. Used individually, the elegant nerine is popular for line or parallel design arrangements. Bunched together, these flowers are superb for creating very clean and contemporary designs, such as this living topiary.

1 Tie the nerines together with wired florist's tie just under their flower heads, then trim the stems so that they are all the same length. Next wrap the stems with soft aluminium wire, which will keep them all together.

2 Place a piece of florist's fix onto the bottom of the pin holder and firmly stick it into the centre of the glass dish. Position the nerine stems securely into the pin holder. Place dianthus and rose flower heads and individual cymbidium flowers in the dish to create a patchwork of colour and different textures at the base of the display. Weave more aluminum wire around these flowers so that the eye is drawn from the base to the nerine ball at the top of the design. Top up the dish with water mixed with flower food and mist the nerine heads.

Lichens and roses

The inspiration for this horizontal low arrangement came from a bundle of twigs covered in lichen. Lichen consists of a fungus growing in close association with an alga, and is sold commercially either on branches or as moss. Lichens epitomize the wilderness where they can be found – most are highly sensitive to air pollution and so very few are found near industrial sites or urban centres. Lichen moss tends to grow well in mountainous regions, and so thrives in Scandinavia and in the state of Washington in the USA. Traditionally used to dye wool, lichen is extremely slow-growing and so should not be gathered from the wild.

The moss that has been used in this display is commonly known as reindeer moss and, as the name suggests, it provides part of the reindeer's diet. The natural colour is grey and it is very spongy, which makes it great to use for texture in an arrangement, or as a base to hide the mechanics of the display, as here. I also love to use the textured twigs in festive Christmas wreaths and other arrangements, when its seasonal association with reindeer makes it even more appropriate. The moss is also often used to cover the soil in planted designs.

For this simple and natural flower design, the pale texture of the lichen twigs suggested a very neutral colour scheme. The collective name for colours that have a very weak chroma and are therefore quite "natural" is achromatic. These colours are grey, beige, stone, cream, and white – and in this case I have extended the range to include pale pink. Colour set against mid-grey is always seen at its truest because it does not absorb any colour from the plant material surrounding it. This makes the grey lichen a perfect base for the pastel shades of these roses, which normally would be of too weak a hue to inspire me.

To create this arrangement, fill a very shallow dish with soaked florist's foam about 1in (2.5cm) thick. Pin the lichen twigs into the foam in lines using hairpin stub wires, then add the roses. Fill any gaps with snowberries, placing them throughout to give movement to the overall design.

Ingredients

Roses (*Rosa*)
'Candy Bianca'
'Metallica'
'Xtreme'

Other flowers & foliage
Bundle of lichen twigs
Pink snowberries
(*Symphoricarpos* 'Pink Pearl')

Other materials
Shallow, almost flat dish
Florist's foam
Hairpin stub wires

Cinnamon candle centrepiece

Square arrangements look great on round tables and have a contemporary feel. Cinnamon sticks are a lovely natural and aromatic material with which to edge an arrangement: I use masses of them for festive-season decorations and also in floral designs for weddings. Reeds or twigs could be substituted for the cinnamon sticks, if you wish: if you are wanting a green edge to a design, you could use equisetum. Or why not try spray-painting twigs gold or silver?

Ingredients

Flowers & foliage
10 bicolour roses
(*Rosa* 'Illusion')
10 coffee cream roses
(*Rosa* 'Metalica')
10 tea brown roses
(*Rosa* 'Xtreme')
10 peachy cream roses
(*Rosa* 'Vendelle')
10 pale pink roses
(*Rosa* 'Heaven')
10 stems of lady's mantle
(*Alchemilla mollis*)

Other materials
Designer board florist's foam
Bundle of long cinnamon sticks
Hot glue gun
6 taper candles 18in (46cm) long

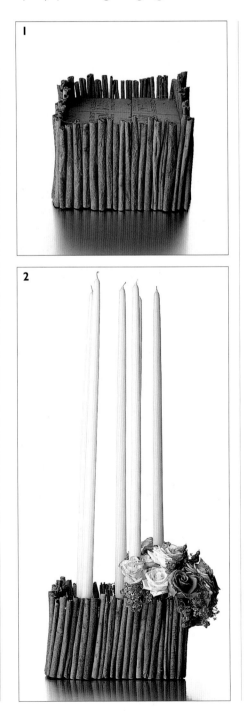

1 Cut an 8 × 8in (20 × 20cm) square from a sheet of florist's designer board. These are large sheets of florist's foam backed with polystyrene. Originally designed to be used mainly for sympathy work, they can be trimmed and cut for a multitude of uses. The foam soaks up water, while the polystyrene side remains dry.

Cut the cinnamon sticks just longer than the height of the block and, using a hot glue gun, stick them upright around the sides. Leave the glue to cool and thoroughly dry.

2 Submerge the whole foam block in water until the air bubbles stop rising, then remove it from the water.

You can now begin to position the flowers. Designer board does not have very deep foam, so you will need to cut the stems of the flowers fairly short. Starting on one side of the block, add a little of the green lady's mantle and then some roses. Mix up the roses so there is a subtle mix of the creams, pink, tea brown, and the bicolour roses. (The 'Illusion' rose used here is a bicolour rose that has been hybridized so that it has many different shades within the one variety. These can range from a greeny cream to very pale pink.) Add the candles as you go so that they sit deep within the flowers. Remember that even in a square design like this, all the plant material should radiate from a central point in the arrangement. When you have finished, mist the flowers.

Dancing anthuriums

Anthuriums are very bold flowers that tend to evoke strong feelings in people. Whether you love them or hate them, they are very useful flowers for floral design — they are both durable and versatile — and now are available in an astonishing number of varieties. Because of their longevity, they are perfect for floral contract work, and you will often find them on the reception desk of a landmark building or in a hotel foyer. One of my favourites is the green 'Midori', which lasts about twenty days and is normally around 5½–6¼in (14–16cm) in size. 'Cognac' and 'Terra' are both, as you would expect, a gorgeous warm brown colour and can last for more than thirty days. 'Rapido', the pinkest of all the anthuriums, can outlive most of the other pink varieties to give forty days of blooming pleasure. Staggeringly, the green and pink bicolours 'General' and 'Baron' often make the late forties, while 'Sultan' lives for more than fifty days. The inflorescence of an anthurium is a large spathe with the flowers on the blunt-ended spadix — the part that makes them the butt of many jokes!

Anthuriums are sold in boxes, each containing about 12 flowers, according to their size. Most varieties are around 4¾in (12cm) wide, but they come in many different sizes. Their very distinctive shape makes them useful for contemporary and minimalist designs. Smaller anthuriums — around 1¼–2in (3–5cm) wide — are often sold as mini-anthuriums in either mixed or single variety boxes. These are the dainty flowers that were used for this delicate design.

First, tape a small block of soaked florist's foam to the top of each of the metal candle stands. Group the candle stands together in a pleasing formation. Add cyclamen leaves to the foam to disguise it, then arrange the anthuriums, making sure that they do not look too crowded. Finally, add some montbretia seed heads to give movement to the arrangement.

Ingredients

Mini-anthuriums (*Anthurium*)
'Midori'
'Acropolis'
'Cheers'

Other flowers & foliage
Cyclamen leaves
Montbretia seed heads
(*Crocosmia* 'Lucifer')

Other materials
Florist's tape
Florist's foam
5 simple metal candle stands

Anthurium 'Midori'

Rose bowls

My first ever arrangement using plant material inside a vase was a competition piece that was judged by one of my own personal floral heroes, the talented floral decorator Kenneth Turner. The top prize-winning design at this competition used burgundy-striped tulips and ranunculus inside a huge glass globe, and this started a whole new exploration for me of designing arrangements inside the vase. On reflection, I learned two very important lessons from this "win". Firstly, that an instinctual feeling for a design, even an extremely simple one, often leads to the best result, and that overworking an idea can produce a more "clever" but less attractive design. Secondly, that all fashions, even in the plant world, do come around again with a slightly different twist. During the Victorian era the floral fashion was to arrange flowers under glass domes, neatly and very precisely, or to grow exotic plants in glass terrariums of elaborate architectural proportions. In the 1970s there was a revival of this craze and the bottle garden became all the rage, while during the 1990s the trend was to display plants in handsome terrariums.

During an interview with a journalist I was once asked a simple question: whether the vase or the flowers come first in my inspiration process. The truth is that it depends. When designing floral arrangements for our own homes we tend to buy flowers for vases we own, for a specific site, or to fill a space, and so the vase is central to our choices. In the case of these very beautiful vases – created by one of my favourite glass artists, Christopher Williams – the pattern and the exquisite colours of the glass suggested an arrangement that would not overpower the work of the glassmaker. These two very striking arrangements also demonstrate that repeating a design and showing two together enhances the display's effect. This "contained" style of flower arranging suits current trends in home decoration and interior design, and provides a very intimate and understated table decoration.

To create this design, simply float rose heads in an inch of water, cutting the rose head off the stem about half an inch (1.5cm) below the calyx.

Ingredients

Roses (*Rosa*)
'Coolwater'
'Aqua'

Other materials
2 round glass bowls

Woven phormium cube

The skill of weaving leaves to create baskets, mats, and even hats entranced me on my first trip to Thailand, and inspired me to create this design. Originally I made it for a fortieth birthday party, where the host was from New Zealand and wished to incorporate some flowers from her homeland into her very British celebrations in her heart of England garden. You can use small staples to help keep the leaves together if you find this weaving requires too much patience.

Ingredients

Roses (*Rosa*)
6 stems of each of the following:
'Aretha'
'Grand Prix'
'Nicole'
'Ruby Red'

Other flowers & foliage
Bundle of New Zealand flax
(*Phormium tenax*)
Camellia leaves
13 gerberas (*Gerbera* 'Ruby Red')

Other materials
Staple gun
Blocks of florist's foam
8in (20cm) glass cube vase
Stub wires

1

2

3

1 Lay three flax leaves down on their sides, next to each other and pointing away from you. Start to weave another leaf across them horizontally. If you wish, you can staple the leaves together with tiny staples to keep them in position as you build up the design. Weave three more leaves through the original three to form a mat.

2 When you have completed four mats in this way you are ready to fill the vase. First place two soaked blocks of florist's foam into the the vase, then position a mat between the foam and the glass on each side, trimming it to the exact size as you do so. Top up the vase with water. Add the glossy camellia leaves to establish the shape of the arrangement.

3 Next add the gerberas, making sure that they are all of a similar height and that they face in all directions. Then add some twisted flax leaves to the arrangement by bending them and securing them into the foam with a double leg-mount. (Flax is tough and the leaves will outlive the flowers even after this treatment.) Finally, add the roses in groups, using more flax leaves around each small bunch to create mini bouquets.

Strelitzia ring

The inspiration for this arrangement came, unusually, from a bridegroom who was organizing his own wedding arrangements. He had decided on the venue and wanted a tall table display that included candles but that would not obscure the guests' view. He also adored strelitzias – birds of paradise – and so wanted them to be incorporated. After a while mulling all these wishes over in the workroom, we came up with this combination. We are still making this design.

Ingredients

Flowers & foliage
Galax leaves (*Galax aphylla*)
Camellia
Ivy berries (*Hedera helix*)
Bunch of red skimmia
(*Skimmia japonica* 'Rubinetta')
Privet berries (*Ligustrum*)
9 orange gerberas
(*Gerbera* 'Mystique')
9 purple tracheliums
(*Trachelium caeruleum* 'Lake
Superior')
6 nutans
(*Leucospermum cordifolium*)
6 ornamental cabbages
(*Brassica oleracea* 'Corgy Dark
Carmine')
9 'Naranga' roses
15 dahlias
(*Dahlia* 'Black Knight')
5 birds of paradise
(*Strelitzia reginae*)
Stem of wild rose hips
(*Rosa canina*)

Other materials
14in (35cm) florist's foam ring
Straight-sided glass bowl (about
12in/30cm in diameter)
Florist's fix
2 1/2in (6cm) pin holder
Nuts or stones

1 Place the soaked ring around the glass bowl and then shave off the top right angle of foam so that the ring edge is rounded. Place a piece of florist's fix on the underside of the pin holder and position this in the centre of the glass bowl. (The more you rub florist's fix in your hand, the more sticky it will become.) Then begin to place the foliage in groups around the edge, starting with the camellia, then adding the galax leaves.

2 To ensure that the plastic base of the ring will not be visible when the display is placed on a table, bend the galax leaves over the edge and outward. Include some berries for texture and interest: here I have used skimmia, ivy berries, and privet. Make sure that you have covered the foam and that the foliage does not droop over the edge of the glass bowl – trim any pieces as necessary. Turn the ring to check its appearance from every angle.

3 Next, add the flowers to the foam ring in strong textural groups. Make sure that some are angled upward and that other groups face outward – these will be the most obvious ones when the arrangement is viewed by guests sitting at the table. When the ring is complete, place the strelitzias onto the pin holder and fill the bowl with stones or, as here, with nuts. Finally, wind the stem of rose hips around the strelitzia stems.

Leucospermum cordifolium 'Tango'

Carnations in a Savoy cabbage

I love the glaucous colour and tactile texture of Savoy cabbages. Arrangements using them are simple to make and they look great placed on a table top or on a cloth. I also often arrange them on a round mirror surrounded by candlelights. Three Savoy cabbages filled with roses also look good around a central candle. If the floral foam is moistened regularly and the cabbage kept in a cool place, the arrangement can last for up to ten days.

Ingredients

Flowers & foliage
Savoy cabbage (*Brassica bullata*)
Trailing red love-lies-bleeding (*Amaranthus caudatus* 'Albiflora')
Japanese privet (*Ligustrum japonicum*) with berries
Grape hyacinths (*Muscari armeniacum*)
Carnations (*Dianthus* 'Scia' and 'Pierrot')

Other materials
Small sheet of plastic (to line cabbage)
Block of florist's foam
Florist's wire

1 Trim the base of a fresh Savoy cabbage so that it sits flat. Now cut out the middle of the cabbage, leaving an outer rim about .1 in (2.5cm) thick all around. Line the cabbage with plastic, then place a small square of moistened floral foam in the middle. Trim it so that it sits snugly inside the cabbage.

2 Arrange groups of love-lies-bleeding and privet berries in small clumps in the middle of the cabbage. For this arrangement, the only foliage is on the privet because the cabbage leaves provide the remainder. The deep-red love-lies-bleeding flowers bring out the colour in the carnations and their plumes give movement to the arrangement.

3 Now add groups of grape hyacinths. Placing flowers in clumps suits a low and textured approach to flower arranging, so choose your material for contrasts in texture and shape. Make sure that the colours and shapes of the flowers near the cabbage leaves are in sympathy with them and that no ugly patches of bare floral foam are showing through the flowers.

Finally, add clumps of carnations to the arrangement (right). Press the cabbage leaves together to hold everything in place. If necessary, you can pin the outer leaves to each other with florist's wire bent into a U-shape to aid stability, but take care not to puncture the plastic lining when doing so.

Dianthus 'Dark Pierrot'

Textural hand-tie

The combination of flowers selected for an arrangement is key to the success of the design. I love to use vibrant colours, but I also adore textural and tactile flowers and foliages such as those I have chosen for this very compact hand-tie. The natural surfaces of plant materials offer enormous variety of textures; from the soft petals of peonies, roses, and carnations to the hard structural form of seed heads, such as those of lotus, poppies, and pine cones. Small flowers, such as daisies, violets, and masterwort (Astrantia), are sometimes best arranged in groups or clusters – they will have more impact if used in greater volume. Flowers that have a distinctive form, such as strelitzia, eremerus, and kniphofia, would be inappropriate for this kind of round design, although they might be useful in a vegetative textural design.

For this arrangement I have used many simple and composite shaped flower heads, including carnations, whose petals are in clusters, and leucospermums, whose many arched pistils form the decorative value of the flower. But for me, celosias are the ultimate textural flowers, with their branched feathery form or soft comb inflorescences.

When an arrangement uses masses of plant material together in order to create a firm, closed surface it is referred to as a "textured design". In such a display, the flower heads take on their own identity, released from their vegetative context. As some of the flowers chosen for this one, such as the leucospermums and leucadendrons, have heavy woody stems and large dominant heads, it is imperative that the other flowers and foliage chosen can compete, and that there is an equal density in colour and texture throughout the arrangement. This creates a patchwork of intense shapes and colours in which each flower head contributes to the total. (For more on hand-ties see Techniques, page 177.)

Ingredients

Flowers & foliage
Leucospermum cordifolium 'Green'
Leucospermum cordifolium 'Red Sunset'
Leucospermum cordifolium 'Sunrise'
Leucadendron 'Flora Bush'
Carnations (*Dianthus* 'Ceram')
Baubles (*Berzelia galpinii*)
Calla lilies (*Zantedeschia aethiopica* 'Chianti')
Celosia
(*Celosia argentia* 'Bombay Pink')

Leucospermum cordifolium

Carnation dome

Many simple geometric shapes work well as topiary forms — cones, pyramids, and spheres are all often used, as well as domes like this one. These shapes can be encountered in nature in inflorescences, leaf forms, seeds, and fruits. The sphere — one of the most commonly occurring natural forms — is seen in seeds, fruits, vegetables, and plants as well as flower heads. This decorative form can be given many treatments: hanging, it can make a huge decoration for a hall or marquee; placed on a trunk it becomes a topiary form for a table or to line an aisle; as a round sphere it is more often used as a dried decoration for the home or as a festive accessory. Massed domes or spheres of a single type of flower have become popular in all kinds of floristry over the last decade, particularly for weddings. These simple shapes work well with uniformly shaped flowers such as roses and carnations. As the latter are less expensive and have larger heads, they are better value to work with.

This simple arrangement is constructed by hand-tying the carnations into a semicircle. Carnations are an excellent flower on which to practise your hand-tying technique as the stems are straight, which makes them easier to use. Because the stems are quite weak, you also have to hold them quite loosely in your hand — an excellent habit to adopt because it helps you to get a better shape.

To create the dome, start by taking one central carnation between the forefinger and thumb of your left hand (assuming you are right-handed). Add five flowers and twist the bunch a quarter turn. Add five more and repeat. Once you have a central core, begin to add the next circle slightly lower so that you begin to build up the dome shape. When you have completed the dome, carefully tie the bunch with wired-edged tape. Add circles of dogwood to a round vase and top it up with water. Place the carnations in the top of the vase and add a swirl of bear grass to the edge to give the arrangement movement and soften the effect.

Ingredients

Flowers & foliage
Carnation (*Dianthus* 'Clove')
Red dogwood shoots
(*Cornus alba* 'Elegantissima')
Bear Grass
(*Xerophyllum asphodeloides*)

Other materials
Straight-sided glass vase
Wire-edged tape

Dianthus 'Clove'

Christmas twig centrepiece

Twig wreaths can make the perfect base for a table centrepiece, and this woven silver-birch twig, cone, and moss base is perfect for the festive season. You can make your own twig wreaths in the spring and autumn, when the sap is rising or falling; birch and dogwood twigs are fairly pliable and can be bound with wire. I also like to prune honeysuckle and clematis vines in the autumn; both have lovely dried tendrils, which can be woven into a wild and natural ring.

Ingredients

Flowers & foliage

Handful of sphagnum moss
(*Sphagnum auriculatum*)
A few ivy trails (*Hedera helix*)
2 bunches of red anemones
(*Anemone coronaria* 'Marianne Red')
Bunch of red skimmia
(*Skimmia japonica* 'Rubella')
20 'Black Bacarra' roses
Variegated holly
(*Ilex aquifolium*)
Bunch of privet berries
(*Ligustrum obtusifolium* 'Aurea Marginata')

Other materials

Plastic bulb bowl
Block of florist's foam
Florist's tape
Twig and cone wreath
0.90mm wire

1 Fill a plastic bulb bowl with soaked florist's foam so that it stands at least 1in (2.5cm) above the top of the bowl. Secure it in position with florist's tape. Fit the bowl inside the twig wreath, again using tape to secure it. Fill the bowl with water mixed with flower food. (Flower food is useful not only in a vase, but also to enhance the life of arrangements in foam.) Add small pieces of green sphagnum moss to the wreath to give it a natural appearance.

2 Place the ends of the ivy trails into the florist's foam so that they can take up water, then weave the ivy through the wreath. The aim is to make it look as though it is growing through the twigs as it would on a tree trunk. Trail ivy around the edge of the pot to hides the mechanics, but make sure that you can still see the foam. You may want to trim off the hard edges of the foam in order to give it a more natural, rounded shape.

3 Place the anemones in a group in the centre of the foam, then edge them with the red blooms of *Skimmia japonica*. Next insert the 'Black Bacarra' roses in a concentric circle around the skimmia, then add a circle of variegated holly and one of the black privet berries. Wire the waxed and sugared pears by placing a 0.90mm wire through the widest part of each pear and twisting the two ends together to form a mount. Finally, place the wired pears around the edge of the berries.

Anemone coronaria
'Marianne Red'

Carnation swirl

Beautiful carnation flowers are avaialble nowadays to growers and hybridizers everywhere, and in fact have become among the most widely available in the world. Disappointingly though, the fact that they are so widespread has made them less attractive to some, and they often receive a rather negative press. However, I am of the firm belief that all flowers have their own intrinsic beauty, which is often enhanced by using them in a holistic way. I adore standard carnations because they are multi-petalled, which means that their large heads, with their serrated or dentated petals, create a great block of colour in a display. I often begin a design from an individual flower, and carnations are very good for textural arrangements. En masse they take on a new shape and form and create a new dynamic. At its most basic, a textural arrangement of carnations can be simply a group of flowers of the same colour formed into a dome or sphere, but they also work well in more complicated geometric designs. Many new varieties of carnation appear each year; my favourites at the moment are the coffee-coloured 'Cappuccino' and the pale green 'Prado'.

Ingredients

Carnations (*Dianthus*)
'Charmeur'
'Scia'
'Clove'
'Dark Pierrot'
'Oliver'

Other flowers & foliage
Laurel (*Laurus nobilis*)
Eucomis (*Eucomis bicolor*)
Steel grass
(*Xanthorrhoea preissii*)

Other materials
12in (30cm) diameter straight-sided bowl
Double-sided sticky tape
Florist's foam

My inspiration for this arrangement was the eucomis flower. I wanted to show the unique beauty of its shape, which most resembles a pineapple. It needs to be seen from all angles and in its entirety so perfectly suits the central area of this display, where it becomes the focus of attention. There is a huge range of colours within the eucomis flower, and these hues have been accentuated by using carnations of matching tones. This is principally a monochromatic colour scheme with the addition of green foliage. The arrangement was created using a 12in (30cm) diameter straight-sided bowl that was covered with double-sided sticky tape. Laurel leaves were then stuck to the edge in a diagonal pattern. Graduated circles of carnations were arranged into soaked florist's foam around the central eucomis. To give the arrangement movement, grass was added to swirl around it, drawing the eye from the carnations and to the eucomis.

Dianthus 'Rosa Monica'

Rose square

Roses are incredibly versatile flowers which can be used to create very contemporary linear designs, as seen here, as well as classic blowzy ones. The immense variety of shades and colours available means that all year round you can create colourful patterns with the flowers heads, using them either in lines or in groups. Rose growers throughout the world are responsive to colour trends, and it is very difficult to keep up to date with the names of all the commercially grown roses that are currently available. With more than 300 South American roses and in excess of 600 varieties available at the Dutch flower auctions, the palette available to the florist every day of the year is quite astonishing.

The use of many blooms of a single flower in this design shows very simply the way that contemporary floral designs have "deconstructed" traditional flower arrangements. Although there are no set rules for creating this kind of display, you will need to consider the balance of the colour throughout the arrangement, its scale and proportion, and whether it has rhythm and vibrancy. Following these principles will lead to a harmonious and successful design.

These rows of roses were arranged without florist's foam or tape by working from one corner to the other in diagonal stripes across the Perspex box. For a box this size you will need about 50 heads. Cut each flower head off its stem just below the calyx so that the head sits on the base of the calyx. When you have arranged all the flowers, dribble in just enough water for the flowers to be able to drink without floating. You will need to top up the water frequently.

Ingredients

Roses (*Rosa*)
(from top to bottom)
'Aqua'
'Grand Prix'
'Coolwater'
'Black Bacarra'
'Grand Prix'
'Aqua'
'Pretty Woman'
'Extreme'
'Black Bacarra'
'Aqua'
'Grand Prix'

Other materials
12in (30cm) square x 2in (5cm)
deep Perspex box

Vanda orchid tree

Over the years that I have been working with flowers, a variety has occasionally come along that is so striking and beautiful that it almost instantly becomes a sensation. I first saw a vanda orchid when I was working on my first flower book in 1991. For the remainder of that decade it remained rare, elusive, and – when available – very expensive. I was intrigued by both its intense and vivid colour and its markings. By the beginning of the new millennium these orchids had been produced as cut flowers by Dutch cut orchid growers, and they became more affordable and readily available. The exquisite markings are similar to those found on the snake's-head fritillary (Fritillaria meleagris), which inspired Charles Rennie Mackintosh when on holiday in 1915 at Walberswick, in my home county of Suffolk.

Vanda orchids are so stunning that although they can complement other flowers in mixed arrangements, they are even more striking when used on their own. Nature is often a great source of inspiration, and one of my favourite early spring blooms is the almost bird-like blossom of magnolia, which gave me the idea for the arrangement shown here.

The "tree trunk" in this arrangement is made by filling a chunky tall glass vase with twisted hazel and individual vanda heads (see page 108 for tips on how to do this). Hazel is usually thicker, curlier, and stronger than willow, and is therefore more suitable for this display, but as it is also slower growing, it usually commands a higher price. The "tree" is hung with test tubes, which are attached with aluminium wire. Each tube contains a vanda orchid, its individual stem cut long enough to reach the bottom of the test tube so that the flower can drink. Glass test tubes are generally easy to purchase, but if you are unable to find or afford them you could use the plastic phials that the orchids are shipped with instead. If you wish, you could use a hot glue gun and cover these plastic phials with leaves, or even dip them in sand or glitter, to conceal them. Once the display is complete, carefully fill each test tube and the main vase with water.

In winter, when orchids are cheaper and more plentiful, this is a good way of making a substantial design using a few flowers. Other orchid varieties, including Cymbidium, Cattleya, or Paphiopedilum, would also work well in this way.

Ingredients

Flowers & foliage
15 stems of twisted (corkscrew) hazel (*Corylus avellana* 'Contortia')
30–40 heads of purple vanda orchids (*Vanda rothschildiana*)

Other materials
Tall sturdy glass vase at least 40in (1m) tall
30 glass test tubes
Reel of aluminium wire

Vanda rothschildiana

Delphinium urn

To give my arrangements a more sculptural feel I like to fashion my own containers. I am always looking out for new ones and new ideas, but often I will return to classic shapes such as this wire urn. It is important to consider proportion and scale when you are designing a floral display and this one follows very traditional lines. The scale will be dictated in part by the position or use of the arrangement; for example, if you want to make a huge impact in a large space it will need to be as big as possible. In a traditionally proportioned display, the flowers and foliage will be at least one and a half times the height of the container. If you choose to use an urn on a plinth for your design, your floral arrangement should be one and a half times higher than the plinth and urn together. This arrangement shows the visually pleasing effect of these traditional proportions. In any design there is an area to which the eye is drawn, the focal point. This should be the part of the display that is perceived to contain the most interest. The lisianthus provides the focal point here.

To make this arrangement, fit a plastic bucket or container inside a wire urn and fill the gap between the two with mind-your-own-business plants. Place soaked florist's foam inside the central container, then add the delphiniums to the foam. All the stems should be about the same height. Add lisianthus around the rim of the urn to create an area of interest and to soften the edge of the container. You will need to mist the arrangement frequently to keep the plants damp.

Ingredients

Flowers & foliage
Mind-your-own-business (*Helxine soleirolii*)
Delphiniums (*Delphinium belladonna* 'Volkerfieden')
Lisianthus (*Eustoma russellianum* 'Ballet Star' and 'Scirpus')

Other materials
Plastic container or bucket
Wire urn
Florist's foam

Eustoma russellianum 'Ballet Star'

Sunflower vase

This idea for this design literally came out of the waste bucket in the shop! For our weekly contract arrangements I had ordered lots of sunflowers, which I discovered as the week went on had been harvested after a wet or damp spell. This meant that all their petals fell (though the centres were still good and strong) and by the middle of the week we were pulling them out of offices and restaurants all over London. Sunflowers were then at the very height of fashion and we had them in all sizes and colours and many different varieties. At the time we were embellishing vases by covering them with leaves and reeds, and so the idea of using these redundant sunflowers in the same way just happened. The vases became a huge success and were to be found at all the best parties: at a chic Formula One celebration they were filled with complete sunflowers; they were stuffed with giant multicoloured dahlias for a gallery private view; and for an autumn wedding they were combined with masses of deep red gladioli, crab apples, green dill, and seasonal foliage. The moral of the tale is never throw away any plant material until you have thought "out of the box" how you might be able to use it.

This heavy base was created by literally sticking the backs of the flower heads to the vase using a large hot glue gun. You can buy glue guns from home and hobby stores in many sizes: for a project like this I recommend you use an industrial-size one as you need the glue to be thick and very hot for the flowers to stick onto the glass. Once you have completed the gluing, leave the vase to dry for a while before adding flowers and foliage to it.

Because the sunflower heads give such a strong look to the base of the arrangement, you will need to select boldly shaped flowers and foliage that are able to compete with them, or the vase will overshadow the rest of the display. The cardoon — often known as the artichoke — is a statuesque, very striking, thistle-like flower and makes the perfect focal flower in this design. I have accompanied it with dill, rudbeckia seed heads, twisty willow, and yucca leaves.

Ingredients

**Sunflowers
(*Helianthus annuus*)**
'Flame'
'Full Sun'
'Prado Red'

Other flowers & foliage
Artichoke/cardoon flowers
(*Cynara cardunculus*)
Dill (*Anethum graveolens*)
Rudbeckia seed heads (*Rudbeckia*)
Willow
(*Salix matsudana* 'Tortuosa')
Bells of Ireland (*Yucca aloifolia*)

Other materials
Large round vase or container
Large hot glue gun

Techniques

Tools of the trade

Equipment

Although it is quite possible to create attractive flower arrangements with minimal specialist knowledge, the practical techniques illustrated and explained in this chapter will, once mastered, greatly increase the creative scope of the amateur arranger. The more you develop your skills, the more enjoyment the art of flower arranging will afford you.

Whether you grow your own flowers or buy them, the items of equipment – or "mechanics" as they are commonly called – illustrated opposite will help you to arrange flowers and foliage to professional standards. All the items shown are essential tools of the trade for trained florists and, used correctly, will enable the amateur flower arranger to construct ambitious large-scale displays that keep their symmetry, and smaller arrangements in which every stem stays in place. Even the most delicate petals and unwieldy vegetables can hold their own once you have learned the basic techniques of wiring.

One of the most important pieces of equipment is a sharp cutting implement. Scissors or a knife are vital for cutting the ends off all sorts of stems cleanly before arranging them, and secateurs are useful for cutting hard woody stems. If you wish to create a large arrangement using a lot of plant material, stand stems in water while you work to prevent them wilting. It is a good idea to prepare the stems on a large piece of plastic sheeting to protect surfaces and speed up clearing away.

The mechanics of flower arranging can broadly be divided into two sections: bases and supports.

Bases

Hanging baskets provide a useful base for cascading arrangements. Two semi-spherical baskets joined together will make a base for a hanging ball or a large-scale topiary tree – fill the basket with florist's foam or moss and then begin to insert the stems. Half baskets are useful for hanging onto walls, while hanging balls are an attractive option for formal celebrations such as a wedding party.

There are various types of florist's foam. The green foam, which can be soaked only once, must be floated on water (do not force it under). Once the foam has sunk and air bubbles cease to rise to the surface, it is ready for using (following the manufacturer's instructions). Make sure that the foam remains moist by topping it up with water as necessary. Brown or grey foam is used for dried flower arranging, while dry-foam balls are ideal for making pomanders. Both types come in various shapes and sizes, including bricks, rings, balls, cones, flat "designer" boards – which can be cut into any shape – and crosses (for sympathy flowers). Some also have suction pads and can be attached to a wall.

While a foam base is designed to support even the most delicate stems, heavy-stemmed flowers and foliage are best arranged in a base made of medium-gauge wire mesh crumpled into a loose ball and placed inside a container (though it looks unsightly in a glass or transparent one). Medium-gauge wire mesh is suitable for most stems; if the gauge is too small then it will be difficult to insert the stems. Plastic-coated wire mesh protects the stems from tearing.

Other useful bases include plastic trays, bowls, and pew ends or small-spray trays with handles used for church decoration, which are available in various shapes and sizes and often moulded to accommodate florist's foam neatly. The florist's spike or "frog" can be stuck on the bottom of a plastic tray or bowl and a piece of florist's foam then wedged onto the spike, which holds the foam firmly in place. If the spike does not have a self-adhesive base then a small ball of florist's fix – a waterproof clay-like substance – will hold it in place.

Pin holders, usually made of heavy metal, are placed in the bottom of a vase to provide a stable base for inserting stems, the spikes in the pin holder securing them in place. Deeper well pin holders are also available. Flower stems do not benefit from this kind of support, but pin holders are good for creating ikebana or Japanese-style arrangements.

To decorate a candlestick or a candelabra with flowers for a special occasion, start by inserting a candle cup into the hole where the candle is normally placed. Next attach a block of green florist's foam – which provides a large base to cover with flowers and foliage – into the moulded candle cup using florist's tape. Insert a florist's candle holder into the foam to hold the candle.

Supports

Stub wires come in various thicknesses or gauges, starting with very fine rose wire, which is suitable for wiring the most delicate flowers and leaves as well as individual florets or larger flowers for bridal work. (Small blooms wired into a bouquet or a headdress must not be over-wired or they will look stiff and unnatural.) Heavy-gauge wire is necessary for supporting large flower heads and fruits and vegetables.

While stub wires reinforce stems, reel wire is useful for binding them. Very fine reel wire or silver wire is suitable for binding very light plant material and is used primarily in bridal work, for example for adding wired flowers into a bouquet or a headdress. Medium-gauge reel wire is useful for binding moss onto a wreath base, for constructing the base of a hanging ball, or for adding to a garland. You can make almost any shape by sculpting moss with reel wire, including hearts, teddy bears, or other animals. Reel wire is also frequently used for grouping bunches of foliage or flowers into sprigs before adding them to an arrangement.

To supplement the support of wiring you can use pins. For example, to pin a large clump of moss to a base, take a heavy stub wire and bend it into a hairpin or U-shape (see pages 178–9). Smaller U-shaped German pins will hold leaves onto a base such as a wreath or a ball, while pretty pearl-headed pins are useful for pinning a corsage to a lapel or attaching a garland of light trails of ivy to a table cloth.

String, rope, raffia, or ribbon can also be used to bind stems, as can the various types of florist's tape that are available. These specialist tapes are waterproof and come in different widths and colours; dark green tape is least conspicuous as it resembles the natural colour of the stems. Wide tape can be used for securing blocks of florist's foam to a large pedestal and thinner tape for attaching foam to a candle cup. Narrow green tape is useful for concealing wired stems and sharp exposed wire ends, especially in bridal work, while brown tape will conceal wiring on dried flower stems. Double-sided tape is also very useful: I often cover a container with double-sided tape and decorate it with leaves, twigs, bamboo, and seed heads. Transparent florist's tie tape is good for binding a gift bouquet wrapped in Cellophane.

Garden canes of various lengths and thicknesses provide support for long, weak stems, which tend to flop or break. For a large-scale arrangement it is possible to lengthen stems to suit the proportions of the display by attaching a cone or funnel to a piece of garden cane or bamboo with tape, then simply inserting the stem into the cone.

Dry-hard clay, which acts like quick-drying cement, will support the weight of a topiary tree. Fill a sturdy container with clay and insert the "trunk" into it. When not in use, clay will stay soft and malleable if completely wrapped in plastic, but will turn hard when exposed to the air. Dry-hard clay is easy and clean to use and, because it does not expand when it dries, there is little risk of it cracking the container.

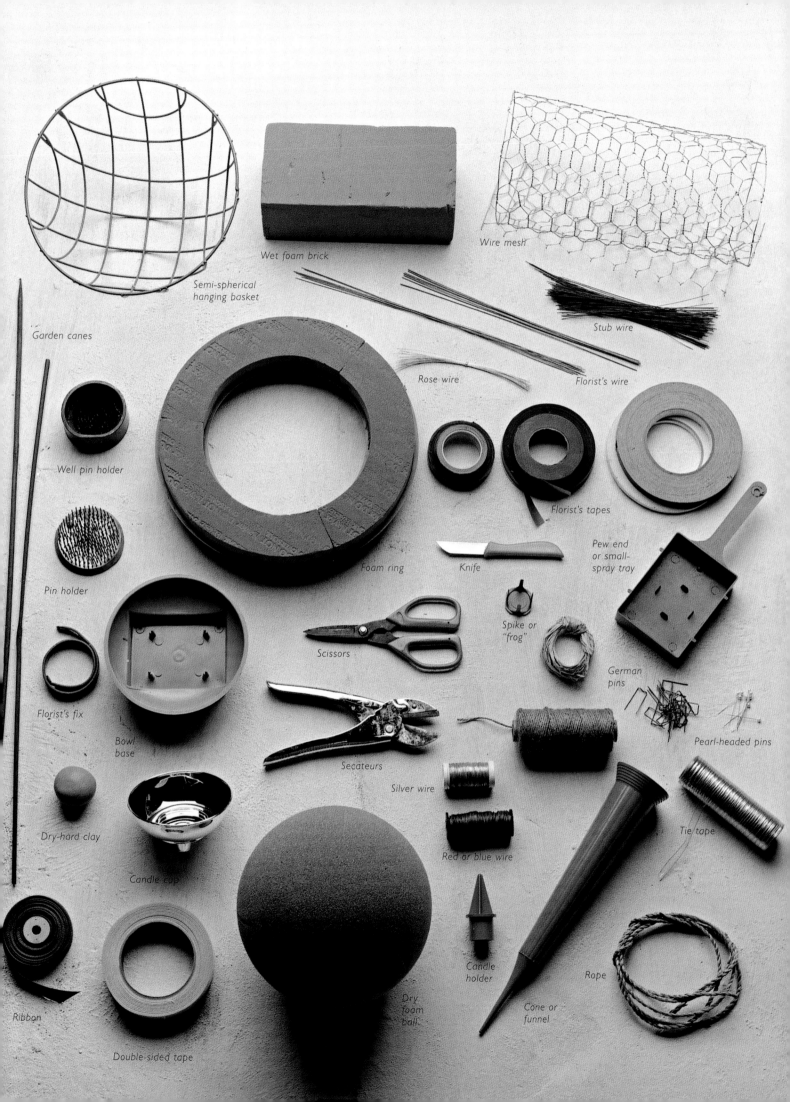

Semi-spherical hanging basket

Wet foam brick

Wire mesh

Garden canes

Stub wire

Rose wire

Florist's wire

Well pin holder

Pin holder

Foam ring

Knife

Pew end or small-spray tray

Florist's tapes

Scissors

Spike or "frog"

German pins

Florist's fix

Bowl base

Secateurs

Silver wire

Pearl-headed pins

Dry-hard clay

Candle cup

Red or blue wire

Tie tape

Ribbon

Double-sided tape

Dry foam ball

Candle holder

Cone or funnel

Rope

Treatment of stems

Before you begin to arrange cut flowers and foliage in a clean container, it is important to prepare the stems in the correct way so that the arrangement lasts as long as possible. First allow the stems to drink in deep water (preferably nutrient-enriched with a commercial cut-flower feed) for several hours. This initial drink revives the plant material and also allows the stems to firm up, which is particularly important if you are arranging in a wet-foam base where stems cannot drink freely.

Always snip the ends of stems before arranging them because this helps them to take up water with maximum efficiency. Different types of stems require different treatments in order to prolong life (see below). A stem end that has lost its green colour – as is common with daffodils (*Narcissus*), for example – must be removed, as the white part will not draw water. Also, you should leave sappy stems such as euphorbias to soak before arranging them, otherwise the oozing liquid will contaminate the water in the container and can look unsightly. Where stems have hard nodules, as for example with carnations (*Dianthus*), make a snip above a nodule to facilitate drinking.

If you find cut flowers are wilting, perhaps after transportation, you can revive them by various methods (see below). Running cool water over the stems and spraying the petals with a mister spray will also help to prevent wilting. You can greatly improve the appearance of tired grey (but not green) foliage by submerging the leaves completely under water. Clean dusty grey leaves with warm water mixed with liquid detergent and polish shiny leaves with a dab of cooking oil.

The tightly closed uppermost buds of a stem rarely open before the lower buds have bloomed and died, so snip them off to prevent them taking water away from the rest of the stem. Remove the stamens from lilies as they tend to stain anything they come into contact with.

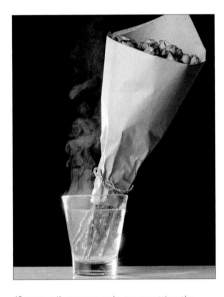

If roses wilt prematurely, try recutting the stems. As a last resort, wrap the heads in paper to protect against steam and plunge stem ends into boiling water for 10 seconds.

Sadly, violets wilt all too quickly. To revive them for making a posy or a small bunch, immerse the flowers completely in water for up to one hour.

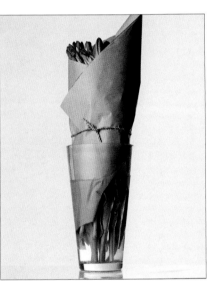

Tulip stems tend to bend. To prevent this, wrap the flowers in paper (which absorbs water) and place in a bucket of water overnight in a cool room.

To condition flowers and foliage, take off the last inch or two of stem in a diagonal cut with a sharp knife or pair of scissors.

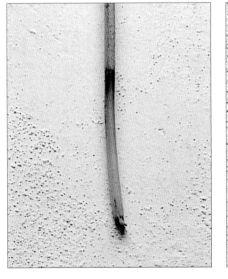

Poppy stems exude latex. Singe the ends with a naked flame to prevent the sap oozing out and blocking the stem entrance.

Do not hammer or smash stem ends – research shows that this damages the cell structure within the stem.

Hand-tie techniques

A hand-tie is a bunch of flowers and foliage that has been arranged in the hand and tied. The most common form is a round bouquet that is designed to fit straight into a vase. A simple hand-tie may consist of just one type of flower or a mix of plant material. They can be massed, mixed, grouped, or even be line designs. Hand-ties are created in the same way that sheaves of corn used to be stacked after the harvest, when the wheat stems were all spiralled to stand on their own stems for drying. In floristry terms, flat-backed hand-ties are the only type that are known as sheaves, and these are used either for sympathy work or hung as decorations for weddings.

A hand-tied bunch of anemones

1 *Anemones, or windflowers as they are also sometimes called, have beautiful cupped heads, which tend to flatten as they mature. To make a hand-tied bunch, choose long stems – these are easier to work with – and make sure that the petals are not more than half open, otherwise the bunch will not last well. Begin by grouping the stems in one hand and add further stems at an angle.*

2 *This kind of bunch is most effective when made with a mixture of different coloured blooms, including pinks, red, blues, mauves, and purples. With one hand, continue to add long stems diagonally to the bunch, holding this securely in the other hand. It is important not to hold the bunch too tightly, so that you retain the spiral shape. Position the heads of the flowers to form an even dome.*

3 *Continue adding more long stems to the spiral until it is no longer possible to hold all the stems in one hand. At this point, tie the bunch tightly with a length of raffia or string at the narrowest part of the spiral, just below the dome of flower heads. Then cut all the stem ends to an even length. If the bunch is correctly made, it will stand upright without support, like a sheaf of corn.*

A large mixed-flower hand-tie

1 *To make a bunch using large flowers with long stems it is easier to cross the stems than to spiral them neatly, as illustrated above. Concentrate on positioning the flower heads and foliage, which should be built up from the middle outward in an even all-round bunch. Start by selecting the longest stems and group them closely together to form the core of the bunch.*

2 *With one hand, add individual stems of lilies, euphorbia, dill (Anethum graveolens), pussy willow (Salix), eucalyptus, and bear grass (Dasylirion) to the bunch, which should be held tightly in the other hand. You can either add the stems to the outside of the bunch or else insert them from above. Build a bunch that is even all they way round as you work.*

3 *When the bunch becomes too heavy to hold in one hand, tie all the stems together tightly with a length of string or raffia at the narrowest part of the bunch, just below the dome of flower heads. Make sure that the bunch is evenly balanced when viewed from all sides. This arrangement does not need to be too neat: allow the wispy bear grass to fall naturally and so break any rigidity of outline.*

Wiring techniques

To be truly creative as a flower arranger you will need to learn a wide range of wiring techniques that will enable you to support and control all types of plant material. Although these techniques may at first appear confusing, you will find that with practice you will acquire the necessary dexterity and expertise to master them.

Florist's wire, which is used to support and lengthen stems, is available in a wide range of lengths, weights (gauges), and colours. Coloured wires are often used in a purely decorative way and are extremely popular in European floristry. The huge array of gauges and lengths of wire can be daunting for anyone starting out in floristry, but the important rule to remember is simple: always use the lightest possible wire for your purpose. The three most commonly used thicknesses or gauges of wire are the light 0.46mm or 0.56mm, the medium 0.90mm, and the heavy 1.25mm (however, in the US the higher the number of the gauge, the lighter the wire). Light wires are good for leaves and delicate heads, while heavier ones are perfect for securing fruits and larger-headed flowers.

Some wires are sold on spools and are known as binding wires. The heavier 0.56mm blue annealed wire is useful for binding moss and foliage to wreaths and is also used in heavy decorative wedding work. The lighter silver reel wires, which range from the heaviest at 0.46mm to the lightest reel wire at 0.28mm, are used for delicate wedding work.

Once you have chosen the right gauge of wire for the job, the next important step is to cover it with florist's tape if it is going to be visible. Taping not only conceals the wire, giving it a natural appearance, but is also very important in sealing the stems, which prolongs the life of the plant material by slowing the dehydration process.

1 Wire a pomegranate by inserting heavy-gauge wire through the skin and flesh of the base, then twist the two ends together. Smaller vegetables, such as peppers, can be double leg-mounted with a medium-gauge wire (see 13). To wire a miniature aubergine, pierce the base with a single leg-mount using a medium-gauge wire (see 2). To wire a miniature pineapple, insert a heavy-gauge wire straight into the base.

2 To wire a pine cone, wrap heavy-gauge wire around the base and twist the wire tightly so that it cannot slip off the cone. To wire walnuts, either find a weak point in the joint of the nut and insert a length of heavy-gauge wire, or coil one end of a stub wire and glue it to the base of the nut.

3 To neaten a rosebud, make small U-shaped pins from fine wire and pin the sepals into the petals.

4 Thread a fine wire through the base of a floret and bind it to the cut-off stem with a double leg mount (see 13) using silver or rose wire.

5 To attach a large clump of fresh moss to a base, bend heavy-gauge wire into a hairpin.

6 To wire a slipper orchid, insert a fine wire into the stem. Hook the wire and pull down into the petals. Secure the hooked wire to the stem with a second wire.

7 To single leg-mount a small flower, take a medium-gauge wire and bend the top 1in (2.5cm) into a U-shape. Bind the U-end and the cut-off stem together with the long end of the same wire.

8 Wind fine silver wire through a delicate flower head until it provides the support you require. Then take a medium-gauge wire and make a double leg mount (see 13) to act as a reinforced stem.

9 Insert a medium-gauge wire straight up the stem of a carnation (*Dianthus*) and hook the end. Pull the hook down so that it is embedded into the petals. Take a second, thinner wire and bind the calyx of the flower and the medium-gauge wire together.

10 Flowers such as gerberas that have smooth, straight stems lend themselves to external wiring. Insert one end of a medium-gauge wire into the calyx and spiral the wire down the stem.

11 This wired anemone is neatened with green tape, which simulates the natural stem.

12 This pygmy amaryllis (*Hippeastrum*) is well supported with a strong wire inserted into its hollow stem. Use a garden cane to support a large amaryllis.

13 The double leg-mount technique is useful for supporting all sorts of heavy flower heads. Double a length of heavy-gauge wire and place the U-end of the wire against the cut-off stem. Wind one leg of the U around the other. This method extends the stem by two "legs" of wire.

14 To wire foliage such as ivy (*Hedera*) for bridal work, "stitch" fine silver or rose wire through the central vein on the back of the leaf. Then join the two wire ends together and twist them around the cut-off leaf stem.

1 *Wired fruits and vegetables, including miniature varieties.*

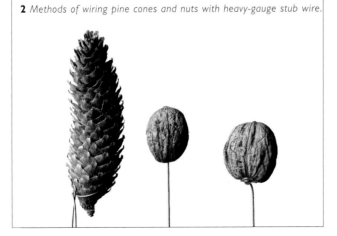

2 *Methods of wiring pine cones and nuts with heavy-gauge stub wire.*

3 *How to neaten a rosebud with pins.*

4 *Wiring a hyacinth floret.*

5 *A heavy hairpin wire holds moss in place.*

6 *Wiring a slipper orchid* (Cypripedium).

7 *A single leg-mounted safflower* (Carthamus).

8 *External wiring on a freesia.*

9 *A hook-wired carnation* (Dianthus).

10 *External wiring on a gerbera.*

11 *A wired stem concealed with green tape.*

12 *Strong wire inserted into a hollow stem.*

13 *A double leg-mounted thistle* (Echinops).

14 *A stitched single ivy* (Hedera) *leaf.*

Presentation

When you arrange flowers and foliage to give to someone, a little extra time spent on presentation will greatly enhance the finished effect. Careful wrapping also protects flowers during transportation. It is best to wrap flowers just before transportation or presentation as they do not benefit from being out of water. Full-blown flowers will not travel well, so use blooms that are in bud or half open.

Most gift flowers require transporting of some kind. If the journey between giver and recipient is a long one, then the cut stems should be kept in a container half-filled with water. If you are transporting the flowers in a car, make sure that the receptacle is firmly wedged in position and cannot topple over. If the flowers are delicate, mould a piece of large-gauge wire mesh over the mouth of a container – this will support the flower heads while allowing the stems to drink. Alternatively you can lay the blooms flat in a box. Do not overfill the box with cut stems or they may become damaged and will tend to smother each other. Wrap delicate blooms in tissue paper dampened using a mister spray to keep them moist. and, if you wish, cover the box with brown paper or decorative gift wrap.

Long-stemmed bunches of flowers transport well protected in a loose spiral of tissue paper covered with gift wrap – this also serves to hide the stems. Short-stemmed bunches and posies look attractive wrapped in Cellophane so that the blooms remain visible. With a small or medium-sized bunch you can leave the flower heads exposed, but it is best to cover a large presentation bouquet entirely with Cellophane to protect the blooms. Pierce small breathing holes in the Cellophane wrapping to prevent the flowers from becoming too hot, which will cause wilting as well as condensation.

Once you have wrapped your posy, bunch, or bouquet the finishing touch is to add a bow. There are many techniques for making bows using ribbons of different widths and types of fabric, or you can use sea grass, rope, string, or raffia. I also like to plait fronds of grasses such as bear grass (*Dasylirion*), to use instead of a bow.

Multi-loop flat bow

1 First select a length of paper or fabric ribbon – here I have used a tartan-patterned fabric one – making sure that it is long enough to form a decent bow. Decide how large you wish the loops of the finished bow to be. Hold one end of the ribbon in one hand and make a loop with the other.

2 Fold the ribbon over itself four times into one loop. The size of this loop will determine the finished size of the bow. Looping the ribbon four times will produce a bow of eight loops; six folds will produce twelve loops, and so on. Take a pair of sharp scissors and snip the end of the ribbon.

3 Once the ribbon is neatly folded, hold it tightly in one hand and, using a pair of sharp scissors, make two V-shaped snips in the middle of the folded ribbon, one on each side. This will form the middle of the bow. Be careful to ensure that the two V-shaped snips do not meet in the middle!

4 Cut a length of the same ribbon to half its width and place it in between the two V-shaped snips. Then tie the strip of ribbon into a tight double knot so that the finished bow is secure and will not come loose. Pull the two ends of the narrower ribbon in opposite directions with both hands.

5 Now start to give the bow shape. With one hand hold the middle of the bow – where the narrower strip of ribbon forms a central knot. With the other hand start to separate each of the four layers of folded ribbon in the original loop. Separate the four loops on one side of the central knot first.

6 Continue to separate the rest of the loops with one hand while holding the middle of the bow with the other hand. Separate all eight loops and shape them so that the outline of the finished bow resembles a pompom. Attach the bow to a bouquet or a bunch with the two narrower strips of ribbon.

To transport cut flowers wrap the stems in tissue paper dampened with a mister spray and place them carefully into a box lined with tissue paper and covered in brown paper. Do not spray orchids or the petals will turn transparent.

This hand-held bunch of pink and blue flowers is wrapped in Cellophane so that the beauty of the blooms is fully visible. The flower heads are uncovered to allow them to breathe and their scent to escape. I have used a wire-edged ribbon, which shapes into a bow.

Three-loop bow

1 To make a three-loop bow, start by selecting a length of ribbon made of paper or fabric – I like to use a wide fabric ribbon. Make sure the ribbon is long enough. Start at one end of the length of ribbon and pinch it in two places using the thumb and forefinger of each hand. The distance between your hands will determine the size of the loop.

2 Transfer the pinched point of the ribbon in your right hand to the pinched point of the ribbon held in your left hand. Hold both pinched points tightly together in your left hand – this forms the middle of the bow. With your right hand pinch the ribbon again to begin to make the second loop of the bow. Keep each loop the same size.

3 Continue to make loops of the same size with your right hand by pinching the ribbon and transferring each pinched point of the ribbon to the left hand so that the ribbon naturally forms a loop. Hold the pinched loops tightly in the left hand. Make a total of six loops in this way so that each half of the bow comprises three loops.

4 When you have finished making six loops of a similar size and all the pinched points of the ribbon are held tightly in your left hand, take a pair of sharp scissors and snip the end of the ribbon after the last loop at an angle. Adjust each of the loops with your right hand so that the bow is symmetrical and rounded.

5 Still holding the bow tightly with the thumb and forefinger of your left hand, take a piece of the same ribbon with your right hand and place it over the middle of the bow at the point where all the loops meet. You will now need to call upon an extra pair of hands to accomplish the final part of making the bow.

6 While you hold all the loops tightly together in your left hand ask someone to tie the short piece of ribbon tightly around the middle of the bow where all the loops meet. Adjust the loops again so that the bow is rounded and symmetrical. Use the ribbon securing the middle of the bow to tie around a bouquet.

Flower Favourites

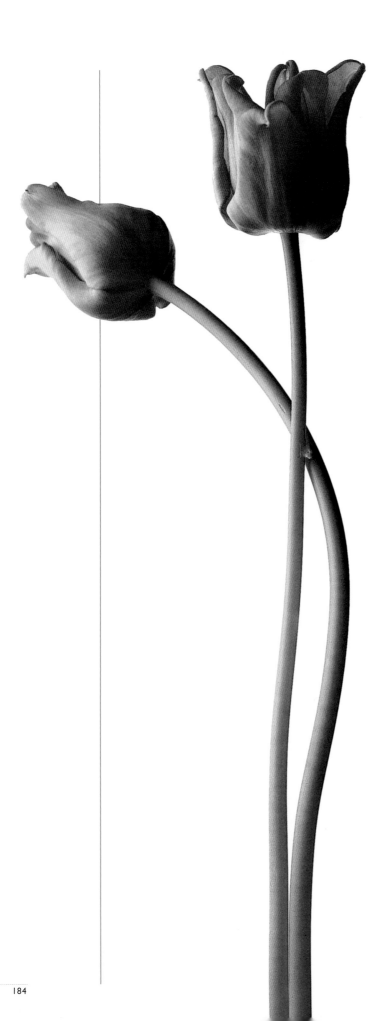

Buying cut flowers

In the flower trade, cut flowers and foliage are the parts of the plant that have an ornamental value when they are removed from the plant. Cut flowers will last a relatively short time (perhaps longer with the addition of special substances), but long enough to be transported all over the world.

The international cut-flower trade is extremely lucrative and so every year more money is invested in cross-breeding varieties, and other methods of refining them, in a constant search for new cultivars and variations in colour and form. Scientific research has helped to extend the longevity of some old varieties, while new flowers are being bred to last longer and be stronger than their ancestors.

This directory will provide you with a snapshot of some of the varieties currently available to the flower designer, and includes some of my personal favourites, many of which appear frequently in this book.

Gerberas are among my top flowers because they are relatively easy to hybridize and are currently available in an astonishing 1,200 varieties. The arrangement of gerberas shown on pages 182–3 was my first well-publicized "deconstruction" arrangement. The photograph of it was made into a poster that was sold in one of the world's most famous Swedish furniture stores, which brought my own style of contemporary floral design into homes all over the world.

A purple-sprayed lotus leaf (Nelumbo nucifera) edges a multicoloured hand-tied arrangement of lotus seed heads, lime-green balls of asclepias (Asclepias fruticosa), dark green folded aspidistra leaves, gloriosa lilies (Gloriosa 'Rothschildiana'), double yellow chrysanthemums (Chrysanthemum Indicum Gr. 'Ellen Geel'), pink peonies (Paeonia 'Sarah Bernhardt'), black ligustrum berries, bright pink germini (Gerbera 'Whisper'), bright pink and fluorescent orange roses (Rosa 'Milano' and 'Wow'), and blue anemones (Anemone coronaria 'Marianne Blue').

Anemone coronaria 'Mona Lisa Orchid'

Anemone coronaria 'Mona Lisa White'

Anemone coronaria

Common name Windflower, from the Greek word *anemos* meaning "wind". *Coronaria* means "crowned" and refers to the crown of leaves below the flower on the stem. The anemone has always been held sacred to love. According to Greek myth, the scarlet anemone was created by Aphrodite from the blood of her dead lover, Adonis, thus ensuring that he would love forever as a flower.

Origin Western Asia and the Mediterranean regions. Anemones have been cultivated since ancient times and were certainly woven into garlands by the Romans. Although they were probably introduced to Britain by the Romans, they became really sought after in the seventeenth century, when their tiny flat tubers would change hands for large sums of money during the plant mania that swept Europe.

Description Herbaceous tuberous plant with deeply laciniated leaves. Petals grow on a crown of green sepals at the top of a bare and elegant stem. These jewel-coloured flowers belong to my favourite flower family of Ranunculaceae.

Colours Purple, magenta, shades of pink, red, burgundy, lavender, lilac, and white. Occasionally in the spring, when these flowers are plentiful, white ones are artificially dyed orange or yellow. The most popular anemones are the rich dark colours, which have black or green centres.

Varieties 'Mona Lisa' is the most common cultivated variety for the flower trade, and its stems are generally about 18in (45cm) long. 'Mona Lisa', 'Marianne', and 'Galil' varieties are all large-flowering types. Although they are available throughout most of the year — except in midsummer — they are at their seasonal best in the spring. The large-flowered varieties grown in Italy and the south of France are my favourites. The best place to see French anemones is either at the Nice flower market or at the huge wholesale market at Rungis, outside Paris, which is well worth an early morning visit.

Vase life Generally between five and seven days, but possibly as long as twelve days if kept at moderate temperatures. Anemones should be bought in bud (but the flower should be fully grown) and they are often packed in paper. Anemones are heavy drinkers, so remember to refresh the vase water frequently. The colour of anemones can be enhanced by dunking the flower head in water before the conditioning process. To condition them, cut off and discard at least 1in (2.5cm) from the stem at an angle and place stems in deep tepid water mixed with flower food. The flowers will bend toward the light, so keep them in an evenly lit space. Once they have been in water they will not travel well out of it, so they are best aqua-packed if you need to transport them. Their black stamens will shed pollen, so be careful when placing these flowers on a white tablecloth or other delicate surface that could be damaged.

Scent The cultivated anemone has no scent, but old-fashioned garden varieties may be fragrant.

Use Prized by flower arrangers for their jewel-like colours, anemones are best displayed in hand-tied bouquets and vases. You will need to arrange them in water rather than in florist's foam because of their thirsty nature. I adore anemones massed together and arranged quite simply on their own, but they also work very well with other spring flowers, such as hyacinths, ranunculus, tulips, and narcissus. White anemones are popular with spring brides.

The jewel colours of massed 'Mona Lisa' varieties of anemones (Anemone coronaria) *are irresistible arranged on their own without any foliage in a low trug.*

Anethum graveolens

Anethum graveolens

Common name Dill.

Origin Not known, but believed to be Asian; dill was certainly cultivated in ancient Egypt. It grows wild in warm parts of Europe.

Description An annual plant, growing to 24in (60cm) in height, dill has bipinnate to tripinnate leaves and rather large umbelliferous fragrant inflorescences of small flowers on branched stalks. The flower head and colour of dill resemble fennel, but the latter grows taller and has a stronger aniseed smell and feathery leaves.

Colours Yellow.

Varieties *Anethum graveolens* 'Mammoth' has one of the largest heads and is considered best for flower arranging. 'Lumina' is another common cut-flower variety and is available throughout the year. 'Vierling' has slightly more blue-ish green leaves.

Vase life Ten–fourteen days in moderate temperatures. The leaves start to go yellow at the end of this period and plants that have been stored will show discoloration on the leaves.

Scent Strongly aromatic.

Use Dill is a useful filler in mixed arrangements and I often use the limey green inflorescences to liven up colour schemes. It also looks great arranged with other aromatic green and flowering herbs such as bay (*Laurus*), thyme (*Thymus*), and lavender (*Lavendula*).

Anthurium andraeanum 'Fantasia'

Anthurium andraeanum

Common name Tailflower, painter's palette.

Origin Rainforests of Colombia, later extensively cultivated and improved in Belgium and France, and now grown worldwide.

Description The inflorescence is a spadix with the unisexual blooms on a heart-shaped leathery spathe. The flowers have fairly short, 16–24in (40–60cm), stems and are graded according to the width of the head.

Colours As well as the original white and red varieties, there are now several hundred others available, including lots of bicolours and novelties. Some of my favourites are the pale cream 'Vanilla', the lime green 'Midori', bicolour varieties such as the red and green 'Amigo', all shades of pale pink, particularly 'Cheers', the bright pink 'Neon', the red 'Tropical', the lilac 'Rapido', the burgundy 'Safari', the light brown 'Terra' and 'Cognac', and the deep rich brown 'Choco'.

Varieties Approximately 200 varieties are now available, some of which are very similar in colour but with slightly different markings; for example 'Cognac' now includes 'Antique', 'Classic', and 'Extreme' varieties.

Vase life Seven to ten days, maybe as long as twenty days in moderate temperatures. Some growers claim that new varieties can last up to forty days and even longer (see page 146). Remove about 1½in (4cm) from stems with a diagonal cut, and place in fresh water with flower food.

Scent None.

Use Best used in hand-tied bouquets and vases and arranged in water rather than florist's foam because of their thirsty nature.

Anthurium andraeanum 'Greenpeace'

Anthurium andraeanum 'Midori'

A colourful tropical tree can be created with lengths of freshly cut bamboo bound together to make a stalk with a large ball of florist's foam impaled on top. I used the hanging heliconia (Heliconia chartacea 'Sexy Pink'), miniature date palm (Pheonix roebelenii) and queen palm leaves (Arecastrum), gingers (Alpinia purpurata), and rattlers (Calathea crotalifera), along with 'Laguna' and 'Sonate'.

Arachnis

Arachnis 'Maggie Oei'

Common name Scorpion orchid. The genus name is the Greek word for spider, which, like "scorpion", alludes to the shape of these flowers.

Origin Cultivated widely in Singapore and Thailand, but originally from Malaysia and Indonesia, where they are also grown for export.

Description Climbing plant, growing up to 16ft (5m) tall and often clinging to trees. Flowers are grouped into single or branched profusely flowering racemes. The 30–60cm (12–24in) stalks, which can be single or branched, are cut and sold in bunches of ten.

Colour Rich, intense tropical colours: red, yellow, tangerine, brown, bright pink, and purple-pink.

Varieties 'Maggie Oei' (shown opposite) and the red 'James Storei' are the most common varieties. The Mokkara hybrids are similar to *Arachnis*, but have larger, more densely packed flowers on sturdier and shorter stems. Popular ones include the orange Mokkara 'Tangerine', the red Mokkara 'Robin' and 'Ruby' ,the bright pink Mokkara 'Patou Siam', and the purple-pink 'Mok'.

Vase life Seven to ten days, maybe more, depending on how long the flowers have been in transit from their homeland.

Scent Slightly musky.

Use Prized by flower arrangers for their jewel-like colours, these orchids are best displayed in hand-tied bouquets and vases. Because of their thirsty nature, you will need to arrange them in water rather than in florist's foam.

Astilbe (Arendsii Gr.) 'Erika'

Astilbe

Common name Florist's spiraea.

Origin The Arendsii group astilbes are natives of China and Korea; those in the Japonica group are from Japan (hence their name). Arendsii group astilbes take their name from the German perennial plant breeder Arends, who first bred these astilbes in 1910, although in fact the Frenchman Lemoine had already crossed these breeds as early as 1895.

Description Outdoor flowering perennial growing to 2–3ft (60cm–1m) tall. The leaves are in various shades of purple and green, depending on the colour of the flowers, which grow in large thick panicles. Astilbes are naturally summer flowering and are plentiful in midsummer.

Colours Various shades of dark red, purplish pink, mid-pink, soft pink, salmon pink, white, and cream.

Varieties There are numerous Arendsii hybrids, for example the cream *Astilbe* (Arendsii Gr.) 'Dimant' and the pink 'Erika'; a few Chinensis hybrids, such as the pink 'Visions' varieties; and some Japonica hybrids (including the white 'Whasington', or 'Washington'), which flower earlier and are generally shorter.

Vase life They will generally keep from five to eight days, but possibly less during hot weather.

Scent None.

Use Great for summer arrangements. They can dry out very quickly, so are best arranged in water rather than in foam, and you will need to top up the vase regularly. In hot weather, aqua-pack them for transportation.

Bouvardia 'Pink Luck'

Bouvardia

Common name Bouvardia.

Origin *Bouvardia longiflora*, *B. leiantha* and *B. ternifolia* are all indigenous to Mexico. The genus is named after the Parisian physician Charles Bouvard (1571–1658), director of the Jardin des Plantes and personal physician to King Louis XIII, who discovered it.

Description A semi-woody shrub that produces branches about 16–39in (40–100cm) long. Leaves are small and pointed and the blooms grow in terminal corymbs of delicate flowers.

Colours Various shades of pink, white, and red.

Varieties The new hybrid varieties are commercially produced in hot houses, mainly in the Netherlands. The main season is from late spring to early winter, but some are available throughout the year. Cultivars include the white 'Arthemy', very pale pink 'Bridesmaid', slightly deeper pink 'Arethusa', salmon pink 'Daphne', and bright red 'Royal Katy' and 'President Cleveland'. The range includes single and double types.

Vase life Seven to ten days in moderate temperatures. Bouvardias are usually sold with special flower food and wrapped tightly to prevent limpness. Leaves have a tendency to wilt in dry air conditions and much research is being carried out to improve their vase life. Royal series bouvardias – there are currently about twenty cultivars – are sturdier and more reliable than other types.

Scent The cultivated hybrids have little or no scent.

Use Bridal work, hand-ties, and arrangements.

Brassica oleracea

Common name Ornamental cabbage.

Origin Cabbages have been cultivated since very early times for consumption, but have only been seen in cut-flower markets during the last fifteen years.

Description The polymorphic species of cabbage, *Brassica oleracea*, is perfect for flower arranging, with its long thick stem, rosette of leaves, and waxy finish. Stems range from 18 to 28in (45cm–70cm). Growers remove the lower foliage before the cabbages are transported.

Colours Various natural varieties range from all green, white, and cream to purple and deep violet colours.

Varieties There are around ten different varieties in production, mainly in the Netherlands. White varieties of *Brassica oleracea* include 'Sunrise', 'White Crane', and 'Corgy White', while 'Sunset' is purple and 'Corgy Pink' paler and more pinky in colour. Ornamental cabbages are available from late summer but are most plentiful in autumn, which is their traditional season. They are now also available from mid to late winter, after which the supply becomes more scarce.

Vase life Generally seven days, but possibly as long as fourteen days in moderate temperatures.

Scent Surprisingly little, but as they age their natural odours do intensify.

Use Cabbages are perfect for large arrangements and chunky hand-tied bouquets. Add a few drops of bleach to keep the water fresh, and change it often to avoid the natural odours associated with cabbages.

Brassica oleracea 'Sunrise'

Callicarpa bodinieri

Common name Beauty berry.

Origin China.

Description An upright deciduous shrub, which grows to approximately 6½–8ft (2–2.5m) in height. The large oval tapering leaves have serrated edges, and the flowers, which appear in early summer, are small and lavender pink. But the plant is mainly grown for its long-lasting shiny bead-like berries, which are deep violet in colour and appear in the autumn on stems about 2–5ft (60cm–1.5m) long. Most stems have branches of the form shown opposite, but some Dutch growers produce plants with very straight stems that have groups of berries all along them.

Colours Violet-coloured berries.

Varieties *Callicarpa bodinieri* var. *giraldii* 'Profusion', shown opposite, is the most commonly cultivated form sold for floral decoration.

Vase life Branches with berries can last up to three weeks and are best treated with a shrub flower food. Do not allow the stems to dry out as the berries will then drop.

Scent None.

Use Excellent for vase arrangements, particularly for contract work or other large designs. They are great for autumn weddings and parties and the berries also look fantastic if floated – I often use them in bowls with candles. The short season of this plant makes it an annual treat, and the extraordinary colour of the berries is often a talking point.

Callicarpa bodinieri var. *giraldii* 'Profusion'

Campanula medium 'Roze'

Campanula medium

Common name Canterbury bell, cup and saucer plant.

Origin The plant was first cultivated in France but it is now grown in all the temperate regions of the world.

Description An outdoor-growing biennial, which has round, branched, and hairy stalks approximately 30in (75cm) tall. The flowers are broad and bell shaped, have short stems, and hang gracefully in large pyramidal stems. Canterbury bells are grown outdoors in the summer, but also in hothouses, so that they can come onto the market as early as late spring. The outdoor-grown varieties are usually stronger than the hothouse-grown ones, however.

Colours White, pink, violet, and lilac.

Varieties There are many different campanulas that are available as cut flowers. *Campanula medium* is available only from early to midsummer. *C. persicifolia* is a similar species in flower at the same time, while the season for *C. pyramidalis* runs until late summer.

Vase life Five to eight days; may be as long as ten days in moderate temperatures. Remove the lower leaves, then cut each stem at a diagonal angle and place it in tepid water mixed with a herbaceous flower food preparation.

Scent None.

Use Summer vases and large arrangements. The multi-headed stem survives better in water than in florist's foam and should never be allowed to dry out.

Cattleya walkeriana var. 'Alba'

Cattleya

Common name Cattleya. The genus was named after the wealthy nineteenth-century British merchant William Cattley, who was a member of the Royal Horticultural Society and possessed a very large collection of exotic plants.

Origin Tropical Central and South America. The genus is now cultivated all over the world, though principally in the Americas.

Description An orchid with pseudo-bulbs that bear two or four flowers in large-flowering cultivars. The small-flowering cultivars bear more flowers – maybe as many as eight on each stalk. There have been literally thousands of hybrids created within the genus and related members of the *Cattleya* alliance.

Colours Many showy, colourful varieties, ranging from lilac to yellow, orange, and white, which are popular for weddings. Bicolours are also common as the tip is usually darker than, or of a contrasting colour to, the perianth petals.

Varieties It is quite difficult to specify individual varieties because this is such a huge family of hybrids. Look out for the *Brassocattleya* varieties for their exquisite scent.

Vase life Seven to ten days.

Scent Slightly to highly fragrant, depending on the cultivar

Use Although they are useful for specimen vases, they are most treasured by florists for high-design work or wedding work because they are extravagant and can command high prices.

Celosia

Common name Cock's comb.

Origin Originally from tropical Africa, these flowers are now grown all over the world. The Japanese developed a lot of the original hybrids, but my favourite varieties are the huge 3ft (1m) tall stems that are now being cultivated in Italy.

Description Half-hardy annual, with a thick fleshy stalk approximately 3ft (1m) tall and a branched feathery flower panicle or a comb-shaped inflorescence as shown opposite.

Colours Various rich colours such as red, purple, magenta, salmon pink, yellow, and lime green, also white. There are some more mellow hues such as the pink 'Cynthia Rose' and the purple 'Century Paars'.

Varieties Celosia in the Plumosa group have one main panicle and pointed plumes. The 'Torch' series is very popular. Those in the Cristata group have a wide, comb-shaped inflorescence. I love the lime-green Celosia (Cristata Gr.) 'Bombay Yellow' and also the other 'Bombay' colours in the Cristata group: orange and pink.

Vase life Seven to ten days in moderate temperatures. Place in a clean vase with cut-flower food. Avoid fluctuations in temperature.

Scent None.

Use I love the texture of the cock's comb varieties in hand-ties and arrangements, and I find the plumes particularly useful for vases and large-scale designs, but it is the vivid colours of these flowers that attracts me most.

Peonies can be used in an innovative ways by mixing them with hot tropical flowers to create a clashing effect. Here they have been hand-tied with yellow yarrow (Achillea filipendulina 'Moonshine'), roses (Rosa 'Nicole Pink'), Celosia (Cristata Gr.) 'Bombay Pink' and 'Bombay Yellow', and pink arum lilies (Zantedeschia 'Majestic Red'). A ruff of anthuriums edges the top of the design, which has been tied with lotus flowers (Nelumbo nucifera) and placed in a globe glass bowl filled with Celosia heads.

Chrysanthemum (Indicum Gr.) 'Tom Pearce'

Chrysanthemum

Common name Chrysanthemum. For several years the florists' chrysanthemum was reclassified as *Dendranthema*, but it is now accepted once more under its old name of *Chrysanthemum*.

Origin Chrysanthemums originally came from China, where they have been cultivated for more than 2500 years. The Japanese frequently used them in their art as a symbol of longevity and happiness. They first came to Europe via the spice trade in the seventeenth century.

Description Very branching woody stems with a leaf shape varying from dentate to lobed. The leaves are greyish green and slightly downy and the flower heads generally stand in plumes, clusters, or as single heads. There are many different classifications: irregular incurved, reflexed, regular incurved, decorative, pompom, single, and semi-double, anemone, spoon, quill, spider, brush, thistle, and even unclassified.

Colours Numerous varieties in all shades except cornflower blue – unless artificially dyed!

Varieties Chrysanthemums are grown under glass all year round and there is a huge range available throughout the year. The annual species that flower outdoors in the autumn are mainly small plants, daisy-shaped and either single or semi-double, closely resembling the Aster family.

Vase life Generally from seven to ten days, though some varieties will last as long as three weeks.

Scent Highly spicy and aromatic.

Use All floristry uses: they are extremely versatile and long-lasting.

Chrysanthemum (Indicum Gr.) 'Shamrock'

Chrysanthemum (Indicum Gr.) 'Reagan White'

Cymbidium 'Alice Anderson'

Cymbidium

Common name Cymbidium orchid.

Origin The ancestors of the large-flowered varieties came from Burma, India, and the Himalayas.

Description Long and short branches with large numbers of waxy flowers in many hues and combinations, always with a remarkable shape and colour. There are large and small cultivars (the latter known as miniature cymbidiums). Flowers are available almost all year round, as they are grown in both the northern and southern hemispheres, though there is generally a break in supply around midsummer and they are at their best in the winter. Their value is determined by the size of the head and the number of heads on each stem, although, as with all flowers, their price is also subject to demand and market fluctuations.

Colours Various, including green, white, pink, yellow, carmine, red, and brown with a beautifully marked lip ("nose").

Varieties A huge assortment of varieties, with newcomers being added every day. For this reason, cymbidium orchids are usually bought by colour rather than by variety name.

Vase life Small varieties from twelve to twenty five days; large ones up to five weeks.

Scent Generally none, though some varieties have a faint scent.

Use Very versatile. Good for weddings and corporate work, and – because they are extravagant and symbolize love – popular for Valentine's Day. Also a good long-lasting cut flower for the festive season.

This bridal decoration uses two stems of miniature cymbidium orchids. The heads have been wired individually onto a wreath of clematis decorated with ivy (Hedera helix).

Cynara scolymus

Common name Globe artichoke; Cardoon flower. *Cynara* is the Latin word from the Greek *kunara*, the name for a sort of artichoke. *Scolymus*, from the Greek *skolumos*, was the name for a thistle-like plant with an edible receptacle, a possible ancestor of our edible artichoke.

Origin The flower does not exist in the wild and is generally believed to have originated from the cardoon (*Cynara cardunculus*). This plant was cultivated in the Mediterranean by the Greeks and the Romans, who imported them from North Africa. In northern Europe it was considered an aristocratic vegetable and cultivated from the sixteenth century, when it was a favourite of the English King Henry VIII, who allegedly prized it for its aphrodisiac qualities. Until the 1960s, the globe artichoke was confined to the vegetable patch, but in the last forty years it has become highly regarded for its appearance too, and has found its way into fashionable flower borders. In the last twenty years it has been cultivated for its flowers, which last a long time and are also very handsome when dried.

Description An outdoor flowering perennial, which can reach a height of 6½ft (2m). The stems are grooved and it has very large pinnate and prickly dentate leaves, which are greyish on top with a silvery white underside. The flower heads are approximately 6in (15cm) in diameter. They have large receptacles, which become pulpy and can be eaten as a vegetable. The triangular bracts have sharp points and are thicker at the base. The inflorescence consists of tubular flowers.

Colours Greyish green leaves and thistle-like, lavender-coloured flowers.

Varieties *Cynara cardunculus* varieties are cultivated for their purple flowers. *C. scolymus* are great as textural rosettes and are grown both for decoration and as a vegetable; varieties include 'Green Globe', 'Gros Vert de Laon', and 'Violetto Precoce'.

Vase life Approximately three weeks.

Scent None.

Use For the flower arranger, they are used in hand-tied bouquets or can make spectacular tall flowers for large arrangements. Their longevity makes them perfect for contract flower work and their architectural lines suit modern as well as massed styles. They are also useful as texture and foliage in the vegetable form shown opposite. Cut with long stems, they command much higher prices for their ornamental value in the flower market than their shorter stemmed counterparts fetch in the vegetable market. Globe artichokes are unusual among vegetables in that it is the immature flower that is eaten. When they are very young, nearly the whole flower is soft enough to eat. When older, only the fleshy bracts are edible, while the "choke" – the thickened receptacle inside – is too tough.

Cynara cardunculus

Cynara scolymus 'Green Globe'

Dahlia 'Sarum Queen'

Dahlia 'Karma Fuchsiana'

Dahlia

Common name Dahlia. The flower is named after A. Dahl (1751–89), a Scandinavian author of botanical works, who was a pupil of Linnaeus, the Swedish botanist who established the binomial naming system that was to be applied to all species, including humans. This naming system is still the one used today, some 250 years after it was devised.

Origin Mexico. The first description of the dahlia comes from a Spanish doctor, Francisco Hernandes, who reported on the plant and animal worlds of "New Spain" (Mexico) in 1615. He called the plant by its Indian name of *acocti*.

Description Dahlias are the most gorgeous members of the daisy family. These herbaceous plants have elongated tuberous roots and thick, hollow stalks. The shape of the ray florets can vary enormously depending on the variety.

Colours All colours – bicolours and bright and dark colours are the most coveted. Because of their vast range of colours, dahlias are great favourites of mine. Red dominates the cut-flower supply, with a thirty per cent share. The deeper burgundy dahlias, such the pompom varieties of 'Black Pearl' and 'Night Queen', are the most fashionable. My personal favourite is 'Arabian Nights': it is one of the richest and deepest reds and has a mysterious impact on other colours when used in mixed arrangements. I also love the purple pompom 'Franz Kafka'.

Varieties Because there is a very short supply period and a huge assortment, dahlias are sold in the cut-flower market by colour, or even in mixed bunches, rather than by variety name. Among the most widely available named dahlias are the decorative 'Karma' series, which were introduced to the cut-flower world in 1996. 'Karma Lagoon' is purple, 'Karma Ohara' yellow, and 'Karma Fuchsiana' bright pink. 'Karma Serena' is appropriately white.

Vase life New cultivars, which are mainly grown from virus-free cuttings rather than from tubers, produce sturdier, uniform flowers that have a longer vase life of between seven and ten days. Outdoor-grown varieties often last a maximum of only five to seven days. Vase life will, of course, depend on the cultivar and the temperature at which they are kept. Dahlias were once a predominantly autumn product, but their growth in popularity has convinced many growers to sow them under glass, so they are now available from mid-spring right through to early winter, with supply peaking between midsummer and mid-autumn.

Scent None.

Use Dahlias are sold when mature to maximize their ornamental value, but this increases their vulnerability during transportation. When botanists discovered dahlias, they thought that the tubers would be useful for our diet and might even rival potatoes, but even pigs turned up their noses at them! Instead they have become very popular as garden flowers for their showy blooms and intense colours. Their popularity as cut flowers over the last ten years has made them fashionable seasonal flowers for the late summer and autumn.

Daucus carota 'Dara'

Common name Burgundy dill, wild carrot.

Origin Europe, Central Asia, Australia, New Zealand, and tropical Africa. This is a variety of a genus with about twenty two species that belongs to the carrot family. *Daucus carota* is the best known and most widely cultivated species in the genus. Grown as a vegetable for centuries, it has only recently been used as a cut flower. *Daucas carota* belongs to the Umbelliferae family.

Description In cultivation, it is considered an annual plant, but in its natural cycle it is really a biennial. This means that the root is developed one year and the flowers and seed heads the second year. It is in its biennial form that *Daucus carota* 'Dara' is useful to the flower arranger.

Colours Dark burgundy red.

Varieties Only one variety of *Daucus carota* 'Dara' is available at present at cut-flower auctions, but it is a new flower, making its first appearance at the beginning of the twenty first century, so new cultivars may follow.

Vase life Five to seven days, maybe up to ten in moderate temperatures

Scent Generally none, but may smell faintly herby

Use Burgundy is a very popular colour and the umbrella-shaped head of this plant makes an attractive filler for hand-ties and arrangements. Its origins in the vegetable patch make it a natural and wild-looking flower that is perfect for informal designs.

Florets of Delphinium *(see page 200)* elatum *'Harlecijn' wired into a headdress with garden roses, alliums (*Allium sphaerocephalon*), poppy seed heads (*Papaver*), and the scented herb oregano – or marjoram – (*Origanum vulgare *'Purple Beauty').*

Delphinium (Elatum Gr.) 'Princess Caroline'

Delphinium

Common name Delphinium; smaller varieties are known as larkspur.

Origin The original varieties came from China and eastern Europe. *Delphinium nudicaule* is native to California.

Description Annual and perennial varieties of tall spires – branches can grow to a height of 4ft (1.2 m) – with close clusters of blossoms.

Colours White and various shades of purple and blue with white and dark centres. There is a limited supply of pink and even orange delphinium hybrids in the Elatum group, but many shades of *Delphinium ajacis* are known.

Varieties The delphinium range comprises three distinct types. The main one, *Delphinium ajacis*, represents around two-thirds of the supply. *D. ajacis* is commonly know as larkspur and is an annual grown from seed. Delphiniums in the Belladonna group are almost exclusively blue; 'Volkerfrieden' is one of the most widely available. The hybrids photographed here belong to the Elatum group. These produce double clusters on stems up to a 3ft (1m) long with sprays of flowers covering nearly 24in (60cm) of the stems.

Vase life Up to twelve days. The addition of flower food will help to prevent colours fading and petals dropping.

Scent None.

Use The smaller varieties are great for large hand-ties and vases, while the hybrids are excellent for large arrangements or bridal work.

Delphinium (Elatum Gr.) 'White Arrow'

Delphinium (Elatum Gr.) 'Cristel'

Dianthus

Common name Carnation, pink. *Dianthus* means divine, and these ubiquitous florists' flowers are so called because of their gorgeous scent.

Origin The Mediterranean region. The original species was *Dianthus caryophyllus*. The species name means "clove-like" and refers to the flower's aromatic scent.

Description A non-hardy perennial grown from cuttings. The garden varieties are grown from seeds as biennials or from cuttings. The carnation comes in standard, spray, micro, and many fancy forms.

Colours An enormous choice of colours, including lots of dual colours in addition to the monos. Pink is one of the most popular, particularly in the spray carnation, with 'Opale' being one of the best known.

Varieties Cross-breeding between the annual 'Chabud' carnations and garden carnations has resulted in the development of many new standard and spray carnation varieties over the past 140 years, initially in the USA and now in every flower-growing area of the world. There are several new varieties added each month, which makes it almost impossible to keep up with their names.

Vase life At least two weeks, which is why carnations are so popular, giving the consumer excellent value.

Scent The garden and border "pinks" are highly aromatic. Sweet william (*D. barbatus*) also has a pleasant fragrance, but the hybrids have had most of their fragrance bred out of them.

Use All aspects of floristry and flower arranging, but particularly popular sold in bunches for home decoration.

Dianthus 'Rendez-Vous'

Dianthus 'Pampa'

Dianthus barbatus 'Barbarella Purple'

Echinops bannaticus 'Blue Globe'

Echinops bannaticus

Common name Globe thistle. The latin name *Echinops* is taken from the ancient Greek word for sea urchin, reflecting the spiky nature of the flower heads before they open up with masses of star-shaped blooms.

Origin The Banat region of Hungary (hence the species name). The similar *Echinops ritro* also originated in Europe.

Description Outdoor flowering perennial that can reach to 2½–5ft (75cm–1.5m) tall. The foliage is grey and the head is fringed with prickles. The globular inflorescence consists of numerous flowers. *Echinops ritro* is similar but has darker green leaves.

Colours Silvery white, greenish grey, grey, and many shades of blue.

Varieties There are about 120 varieties within the genus *Echinops*, which include annuals, biennials, and perennials. One of the most commonly cultivated is 'Taplow Blue', which is pure blue. *Echinops ritro* 'Veitch Blue' is one of the darkest blue varieties and a personal favourite of mine.

Scent None.

Vase life Up to three weeks (but they also dry well).

Use Globe thistles make excellent cut flowers and also dry well, and so are an excellent flower for more permanent arrangements. They are extremely long-lasting and work well in hand-ties, arrangements, or for contract work. Silver flowers are popular and these drumstick flowers add great texture to any style of arrangement.

Eryngium 'Supernova'

Eryngium

Common name Sea holly.

Origin From central and southern Europe to Siberia. The genus *Eryngium* was first cultivated in Belgium in 1567.

Description Mostly perennial plants, reaching to around 2½–3ft (75cm–1m) high, with sharply dentated leaves and prickly dense flower heads surrounded by dramatic spiny bracts, which earn sea holly much of its appeal. Although superficially they may resemble thistles, producing flower heads of tightly packed florets, they are in fact part of the Umbelliferae family.

Colours Varying shades of blue, grey, and silver.

Varieties The genus *Eryngium* has more than 200 species, and breeding work has gone on apace in the cut-flower industry for this textural "filler". *E. planum* is generally one of the taller cultivars with small, pale blue flowers. The largest-headed variety of *E. planum*, 'Tetra Petra', is named after one of the Netherlands' most famous growers. 'Blue Ribbon' is an intensely blue cultivar with multiple bracts. 'Blue Bell' is spikier, while 'Orion' is the deepest blue small-headed variety. 'Supernova' has the largest head and resembles the wild teasel. *E. giganteum* is the largest and is a beautiful silver colour. It is also a biennial rather than a perennial like the rest of the family.

Vase life From twelve to sixteen days, maybe longer in cool conditions.

Scent None.

Use Great for flower arrangements and also for bridal work.

A raft of South African reeds (Cannomis virgata) has been designed to conceal a plastic tray filled with soaked florist's foam and covered with strong groups of flowers – arum lilies (Zantedeschia aethiopica 'Highwood'), poppy seed heads (Papaver), and sea holly (Eryngium alpinium) – edged with hosta leaves and topped with bells of Ireland (Molucella laevis) and Arabian chincherinchees (Ornithogalum arabicum).

Eustoma

Eustoma russellianum 'Mariachi Pink'

Common name Texan poppy

Origin *Eustoma russellianum* is native to the American states of Colorado, Nebraska, New Mexico, and Texas. Since the 1980s, however, eustomas have been cultivated in the Netherlands, and over the last decade the range has been expanded considerably.

Description Biennial from the greenhouse, 27–32in (70–80cm) tall, with branched erect stalks and oval leaves. Petals are inversely egg-shaped with a diameter of about 2in (5cm). Both single and double varieties are available. The flowerbud is enclosed by long, narrow green sepals.

Colours Green, white, cream, dark purple, lilac, pink, and many bicolours, some of which have very subtle markings.

Varieties The 'Mariachi' series takes its name from the Mexican wedding dance, and these double flowers are beautiful and graceful. The 'Echo' series also includes doubles. The 'Piccolo' series has smaller and more plentiful blooms on each stem and a better vase life.

Vase life Around eight days, but with proper care some, such as 'Fuji' and 'Mariachi', can last up to two weeks. As with all relatively new cut flowers, each new series improves on the vase life, and the flower becomes more and more reliable and increasingly popular. Eustomas do not like light humidity, so avoid bright sunlight, where they may be prone to botrytis. The ideal temperature is between 41 and 60°F (5–15°C).

Scent None.

Use Great for vases and hand-ties and also for wedding work.

Gerbera 'Cosmo'

Gerbera

Common name Transvaal daisy.

Origin South Africa.

Description Hardy perennial with single and double varieties. The flower head stands alone at the end of a leafless stem, which grows from a root rosette with a base of numerous leaves 12in (30cm) long. Smaller germini varieties have flower heads from 2½in (6cm) in diameter; in the original gerberas these are 5–6in (12–16cm).

Colours All shades of red, orange, pink, cream, white, yellow, brown, and lilac, some with black or green eyes or double varieties.

Varieties Too many to mention, but two sizes predominate: the large-flowered gerberas and the smaller mini daisies, known as germini.

Vase life Generally fourteen days, though some "super" varieties will live up to three weeks. Hybridizers are now breeding only from stock that has a proven track record of a great vase life. Try to avoid touching flower heads, which are easily damaged, and, as gerberas are particularly sensitive to bacteria, make sure that vase and water are clean. Change the water frequently and use a flower food.

Scent None.

Use Gerberas are the ultimate florists' flowers because of the immense choice in colour, the enormous volume available all year round, their moderate cost, and their versatility – they are useful for all aspects of flower arranging and floristry. The smaller mini daisies are also good for bouquets, smaller arrangements, and for wedding work.

Gerbera 'Anais'

Gerbera 'Ferrari'

Smaller gerberas are known as germini. Here the bright orange 'Paso' variety has been arranged with aspidistra leaves. In the base of this two-tier display are orange-fringed tulips (Tulipa 'Madison Garden') surrounded by South African thatchreeds (Thamnochortus insignis).

This idea was created for a Tex-Mex party. The orange 'Paso', yellow 'Polka', and red 'Salsa' germinis have been wired onto a living cactus.

Gloriosa

Gloriosa superba 'Rothschildiana'

Common name Flame lily or glory lily. The most widely available variety, *Gloriosa superba* 'Rothschildiana', was named after the Baron de Rothschild, who entered this species at a flower exhibition at the Royal Horticultural Society in Britain at the beginning of the twentieth century.

Origin Native to tropical Asia and Africa.

Description This unusual plant is a tuberous perennial vine. It has showy single flowers with recurved petals, which are brightly coloured.

Colours Bicolours of pink and yellow are the most common, but yellow, orange, and red bicolours are also available, though in limited supply.

Varieties The most commonly available, *Gloriosa superba* 'Rothschildiana', is bright scarlet or bright pink, fading to yellow or lime green at the edges of the separated recurved petals. 'Glandiflora' is yellow and 'Simplex' deep orange and yellow. 'Citrina' is the one with the deepest coloration: maroon flowers striped with yellow.

Vase life This fragile flower is often shipped in inflated plastic bags to avoid damage. Remove the flowers from the bag and cut and rehydrate them as soon as possible. If the stems and flowers are very weak and dehydrated, try submerging them underwater overnight to revive them. Although they appear fragile, these lilies can last ten to fourteen days.

Scent None.

Use The short-stemmed flowers, 5–6in (12–15cm) long and sold without leaves, are useful for small arrangements. The branched, longer trailing stems (shown opposite) are great in bouquets and larger displays.

Helianthus annuus 'Moonlight'

Helianthus annuus

Common name Sunflower; so called because the flower head turns to follow the sun. *Helianthus* is derived from the Greek word *helios*, which means sun; *annuus* means annual.

Origin Southern and western regions of the USA. Sunflowers were cultivated by Native Americans for many years.

Description Sowing annuals, with a heavy coarsely haired stalk that can grow to 6ft (1.8m). The large alternate leaves are almost heart shaped and the flower heads vary from 8 to 14in (20 to 35cm) in diameter. Mini varieties, such as 'Italian White', have smaller (4in/10cm) heads.

Colours Predominantly yellow, but also ochre, orange, rusty red, and purplish maroon. Deep yellow cultivars include 'Sungold' and 'Sunrich Orange'; 'Primrose' and 'Vanilla Ice' are paler yellow. 'Ruby Eclipse' is red, and 'Ring of Fire' bicolour brown and yellow. 'Moulin Rouge' is almost black with red tips. Those with strongly contrasting centres, such as 'Sunrich Lemon' – pale yellow with a black disk – have most impact.

Varieties About fifteen cultivars in this genus are popular as cut flowers. These include the classic sunflower 'Snittgold', the small-flowered 'Sonja', and 'Orit'. 'Sunbright' and all the 'Sunrich' cultivars are among those that have been specially developed to shed less pollen.

Vase life Six to ten days. Sunflowers drink a lot of water.

Scent Faint oily smell.

Use Displayed on their own in a vase or in larger arrangements. Small varieties work well in hand-ties.

Helianthus annuus 'Titan'

Helianthus annuus 'Ruby Eclipse'

Heliconia caribaea
'Vermilion'

Heliconia

Common name Wild plantain or lobster claw.

Origin *Heliconia caribaea* originates from the West Indies, but other species can be found in all areas of the American tropics.

Description Banana-like stems bear pointed elliptical leaves up to 4ft (1.2m) long. Relatively short upright inflorescences have two overlapping rows of brightly coloured bracts. Growing from underground rhizomes, these tropical beauties are among the fastest expanding groups of ornamental plants.

Colours Red is by far the most common colour, ranging from pale pink to dark wine red, but green and yellow forms are also available. Sometimes the bracts are edged with green.

Varieties Heliconias range in size from the small *Heliconia stricta* through to the medium-sized *H. psittacorum,* and to giants like *H. caribaca* (shown on thc lcft), which can reach 10ft (3m). *H. caribaea* 'Black Magic' is dark burgundy in colour, whereas 'Gold', predictably, is the most wonderful bright gold colour.

Vase life Three to four weeks.

Scent Generally none, though some varieties smell faintly sweet.

Use The finer, smaller heliconias are useful for contract work – the bold orange 'Golden Torch' and the multicoloured 'Suriname Sassy' are among my favourites. So, too, are the many very striking bicolours. Hanging heliconias are great for large decorations. The pink *Heliconia chartacca* 'Sexy Pink' looks fantastic mixed with tropical foliage.

Heliconia latispatha 'Gyro'

Heliconia rostrata
'Ruiz and Pavon'

Hippeastrum

Common name Amaryllis.

Origin South and Central America and the Caribbean

Description This bulbous plant produces one or two hollow stems of around 20–28in (50–70cm), each with three or four flowers. The dark green leaves appear after the flowers.

Colours Red, pink, salmon, white, and bicolour.

Varieties Two-toned forms include the pink and white 'Apple Blossom' and red and white 'Minerva' and 'Ambiance'. Red ones include 'Red Lion', the slightly brighter 'Roma', and deeper red forms 'Liberty' and 'Royal Velvet'. 'Rilona' is a peach colour and 'Hercules' a deep pink. White amaryllis include 'Christmas Gift', 'Mont Blanc', and the new double variety 'Nymph'. Smaller varieties, often known as 'Pygmy', include the red *Hippeastrum gracilis* 'Pygmee'.

Vase life Eight to fourteen days. Cut stems on a slant and place them in clean water. It is not necessary to add flower food. Placing a bamboo cane through the centre of the hollow stems will help to keep these heavily hybridized blooms strong when they are at their peak. Indeed, without this extra support, stems can sometimes collapse under the weight of the flowers. To ensure optimum blooming, remove the pollen-bearing stamens and individual flowers as soon as they wither.

Scent None.

Use Amaryllis are highly valued as cut flowers because of their impressive vase life. They are good for all kinds of flower arrangements.

Hippeastrum 'Hercules'

Hippeastrum 'Minerva'

Hippeastrum 'Ludwig Dazzler'

Hydrangea macrophylla

Hydrangea

Common name French hortensia

Origin Japan.

Description Shrub with thick twigs and large, fairly thick leaves with deeply serrated margins. The inflorescence is globular, with large flowers. Grows to a height of 3–6ft (1–1.8m).

Colours White, blue, and pink, turning brown-red in autumn, and prized in this state for drying and using in permanent decorations.

Varieties There are about a hundred species in this family, with *Hydrangea macrophylla* being one of the best cut-flower species. *H. paniculata* is cultivated in season as a cut flower, but is less reliable and tends to be used only for weddings, when vase life is not an important consideration. Within the *macrophylla* species there are 500 mophead varieties and around twenty lacecap cultivars, which are more often sold as flowering plants. The increasing popularity of the hydrangea as a cut flower and the immense improvements in its vase life have made this one of the up-and-coming flowers at the beginning of the twenty first century.

Vase life Ten to fourteen days, maybe longer. In their autumn state they can last as long as four to six weeks. Remove most of the foliage to give the flower head the best chance of a long and healthy vase life.

Scent None.

Use In flower arrangements, large and small, and grouped in bouquets. They are good for wedding bouquets and, broken down into florets, they also make great headdress material.

I like to create containers that are part of the design. Here sweet gale twigs (Myrica gale), often sold as 'Gagel', have been wired together and tied with clematis vine around a glass container. Foliage then complements the following irises: blue 'Ideal' and 'Blue Magic' from the Hollandse iris group, and the seasonal black and green widow iris (Hermodactylus tuberosus).

Iris

Common name Iris is a type genus for the family of Iridaceae, taking its name from the Greek God of the rainbow. This is a large genus and there are many seasonal varieties available to the flower arranger throughout the year. The commonly known cut-flower iris, which is available all year round, was created by crossing three parents and creating a florist hybrid called the 'Dutch Iris.' I have also included the widow iris (*Hermodactylus tuberosa*). This perennial is so closely related to the iris that some botanists think it should be included in the genus.

Origin Southern Europe, particularly Spain, and Morocco

Description A bulbous plant, cultivated outdoors and forced under glass. The narrow pointed leaves and the flower stalk are at the same height. The reflexed outer petals have a different colour comb.

Colours Blue accounts for around eighty per cent of cut-flower cultivation. Yellow and white varieties are also available.

Varieties 'Professor Blaauw' is one of the most common deep blue cultivars; others include 'Blue Magic', 'Hong Kong', and 'Blue Diamond'. 'Ideal' is pale blue. 'White Wedgwood' is one of the oldest and most popular white cultivars, and 'Yellow Queen' and 'Golden Harvest' are yellow hybrids.

Vase life About twelve days.

Scent None.

Use Consumer flower, useful for flower arrangements. I don't like them in mixed bouquets because of their shape, but their architectural quality does make them an interesting flower for vegetative or natural designs.

Hermodactylus tuberosa

Iris 'Blue Magic'

Lathyrus latifolius

Lathyrus

Common name Sweet pea.

Origin Central and southern Europe. The scented varieties originate from Italy.

Description This is a genus of annuals and perennials. The climbing perennial *Lathyrus latifolius* is often known as the everlasting sweet pea because of its tenacity, while the annual *L. odoratus* is prized for its wonderful fragrance.

Colours The wild forms are violet, pink, and purple-red. The hybridized sweet peas so loved by gardeners come in an astonishing array of colours, including white, cream, lilac, violet, red, orange, and burgundy, as well as all shades of pink, from the palest to the most shocking, plus salmon and apricot. There are also many interesting bicolours.

Varieties In the cut-flower industry, sweet peas are generally marketed by their colour rather than by their variety. New stronger and longer-lasting annual varieties are being trialed and tested each year.

Vase life Picked from the garden, sweet peas last only around five days, but commercially grown strains last longer and are post-harvest treated to give them a vase life of eight to ten days.

Scent Very fragrant.

Use Good for simple vase arrangements and a popular choice for weddings because of their delicacy. They are also often used for sympathy flowers, as their fragrance and subtle colours have a special place in the memories of many people.

Lathyrus odoratus 'Jayne Amanda'

Lathyrus odoratus 'Noel Sutton'

This wild garden hand-tie is inspired by the midsummer English cottage garden. Here sweet peas have been spiralled with textured spires of pink statice (Limonium suworowiii), Japanese anemones (Anemone japonica), veronica, and dainty foxgloves (Penstemon 'Peace'), and then tied with raffia.

Leucospermum

Leucospermum cordifolium 'Vlam'

Common name Pincushion or nutan.

Origin Western South Africa and the western Cape of Good Hope.

Description Unlike many flowers in related genera of the protea (Proteaceae) family, these evergreen shrubs owe their beauty to their flowers. They have roundish "pincushion" heads with long brightly coloured conspicuous styles.

Colours Many orange, some yellow, and a few that are almost lime green. Favourites include the apricot-yellow 'Fire Dance', 'African Red' with scarlet flower heads, the deep orange 'Flamespike', orange 'Sunrise', and yellow 'High Gold', and 'Yellow Bird'.

Varieties There are approximately fifty species in the genus. *Leucospermum cordifolium* is often also known as a nutan and is available in a range of colours. *L. tottum* produces a denser flower – 'Scarlet Ribbon' is one of the most widely available. *L. patersonii* has bright orange flowers, which are red-tipped, and a very round head. *L. conocarpodendron* is milky yellow in colour, while *L. erubescens* is yellow with a much flatter head.

Vase life A month or longer; however there are large differences in the quality and freshness of supplies.

Scent None

Use Very useful for hand-ties and arrangements, these flowers are excellent for contract work because of their longevity in water and even in florist's foam.

Lilium 'Casablanca'

Lilium

Common name Lily.

Origin Asia.

Description The leaves are short and usually linear or lanceolate. The flowers borne at the end of the stem are solitary or in umbels or panicles, and may be bell-shaped, trumpeted, or star shaped. Some have recurved sepals, producing a "turks-cap" flower. The genus, of around a hundred species, is split into nine main divisions. Of most importance to the cut-flower industry are the Asiatic (star-shaped), longiflorum (trumpet-shaped), and Oriental (tall, scented, and star-shaped) lilies.

Colours All colours except blue; often streaked, bicolour, or spotted.

Varieties The Asiatic group includes the white 'Alaska', cream 'Avignon', red 'Chianti', yellow 'Connecticut King', pink 'Côte d'Azur', and dark orange 'Monte Negro'. Longiflorum lilies are by far the best types and are often referred to as Madonna lilies: 'White Europe' is one of the most common. In the Oriental group, I love the pink varieties 'Sorbonne', 'Mero Star', and 'Acapulco'.

Vase life Ten to fifteen days. It is advisable to remove the anthers to prevent pollen staining the flowers, surfaces, or clothing.

Scent Heavily perfumed.

Use Lilies are most versatile flowers as well as being long-lasting. They are adored for their scent and so are great flowers for the home, weddings and other special occasions, and contract work. They are also very popular for church decorations and for sympathy flowers.

Lilium 'Dolce Vita'

Lilium 'La Rêve'

Here cyclamen leaves and pinkish green heads of sedum disguise florist's foam on a tray. Single-headed lilies (Lilium longiflorum) have been used, then various straight and bent grasses have been added to give the arrangement movement.

Malus

Common name Crab apple.

Origin Asia.

Description A shrub or small tree with serrated leaves. The flowers vary from pale pink to red, but it is prized more by the flower arranger for its autumn-fruiting branches of miniature fruits.

Colours Many shades of red, orange, and pink, plus some gorgeous yellow varieties.

Varieties Numerous crab-apple cultivars have been developed for their flowers and ornamental fruit. 'Professor Sprenger' has pale pink blossoms and green apples blushed with red; 'Red Jewel', 'Red Peacock', and 'Red Sentinel' have beautiful red fruits. Yellow-fruiting varieties are often more interesting for their fruit: 'Wintergold', for example, has very pale flowers but produces a huge number of bright yellow apples. Other good yellow-apple varieties include 'Harvest Gold', 'Bob White', and 'Butterball'.

Vase life In blossom form expect seven to ten days, depending on how tight the blossom is when cut. Fruiting branches last twelve–twenty days.

Scent None.

Use Good for tall arrangements and autumn pedestal arrangements. The fruits look fabulous in vases or pinned into wreaths for Hallowe'en or the winter festive season. Bear in mind that using fruit with flowers will shorten the life of the flowers. However, crab apples can be mixed with other flowers, even for contract work, and together they will have a vase life of around five to seven days, depending on the temperature.

Malus 'Red Sentinel'

Narcissus 'Suzy'

Narcissus

Common name The yellow variety is known as the daffodil; the white variety is often referred to as a paperwhite.

Origin South-western Europe.

Description These bulbous flowers with grassy leaves are split into twelve groups according to their flower shape. The most important of these for the flower designer are the trumpet narcissus (more commonly known as daffodil), the large corolla, the short corolla, the double-flowered, the jonquil, the polyanthus, and the split corolla.

Colours Most of the supply is yellow, but there is also a large assortment of white, cream, yellow with pink, and orange with white.

Varieties Double yellow trumpets 'Dick Wilden' and 'Golden Ducat' are my favourites. For the classic daffodil trumpet shape choose 'Carlton', 'Dutch Master', or 'Golden Harvest'. For paler colour schemes, try the cream with pale yellow 'Ice Follies'.

Vase life Six to twelve days. The narcissus stem gives off slime, which has an unfavourable effect on other flowers. To counteract this, use a special narcissus flower food; alternatively, add a few drops of household bleach to the water when conditioning the narcissus and leave them for twenty four hours before arranging them with other flowers.

Scent Varies, but some varieties, such as 'Geranium', 'Soleil d'Or', 'Cheerfulness', and 'Paperwhite', have a heady perfume.

Use Great for vase arrangements and in small posies and hand-ties; also good for natural vegetative designs.

Narcissus 'Tahiti'

Narcissus 'Yellow Sun'

Oncidium 'Golden Shower'

Oncidium

Common name Dancing lady orchid, Singapore orchid.

Origin Tropical America.

Description This huge genus of sympodial orchids contains more than 750 different species. Oncidium orchids are mostly epiphytic, though a few grow in the ground and some on rocks. Generally they have thick, stem-like pseudobulbs and sprays of very showy flowers, which are usually yellow or brown and borne on large branching inflorescences. A characteristic of most oncidiums is that the prominent flowers have fiddle-shaped lips.

Colours Mostly shades of yellow and brown, though other colours, such as green, red, and magenta may appear occasionally at cut-flower markets and be available as house plants.

Varieties The most popular and widely available oncidium hybrid is 'Golden Shower' (shown on the left). This was first produced by the Singapore Botanic Gardens in 1940 and has become a very popular and long-lasting cut flower.

Vase life Twelve–sixteen days.

Scent None.

Use In vases and arrangements. The longevity of this striking flower makes it a staple for contract work and it can be seen in hotel lobbies across the world.

Massed peonies – 'Sarah Bernhardt', 'China Rose', 'Shirley Temple', 'Knighthood', and 'Duchesse de Nemours' – have been arranged in soaked florist's foam in a shaped basket. I love to mix colours like this and create a patchwork of flowers.

Paeonia

Common name Chinese peony.

Origin Central and East Asia. In China the peony has been cultivated for a thousand years.

Description Most of the species are herbaceous perennials, and these make the best cut flowers. Some peonies are shrubs known as tree peonies, but these are generally not cultivated for the cut-flower market. The reddish stem bears double ternate leaves, which are oval. The simple or multiple flower heads are 4–5in (10–12cm) in diameter.

Colours Shades of white, cream, pink and red. There are also a few coral and yellow varieties.

Varieties Popular ones include 'Festiva Maximia', which is white with a pink centre, the white 'Shirley Temple', pink 'Sarah Bernhardt', carmine pink 'Bowl of Beauty', strong mid-pink 'Dr Alexander Fleming', and the dark pink 'Karl Rosenfield'. Red cultivars are usually hybrids; 'Red Charm' is a beautiful fully double, deep red cultivar with ruffled petals.

Vase life Ten to fifteen days.

Scent Slightly fragrant to heavily scented, depending on the variety. The fragrant white 'Duchesse de Nemours' is a personal favourite.

Use Everyone loves peonies, and these seasonal flowers are prized for all kinds of floristry and flower arranging. They are extremely popular for summer weddings.

Paeonia lactiflora 'Shirley Temple'

Paeonia lactiflora 'Pink Panther'

Papaver orientale 'Allegro Viva'

Papaver somniferum 'Hen and Chicken'

Papaver

Common name Poppy. The genus name *Papaver* may be derived from the word *papa*, meaning Father, because in ancient times the seeds of these flowers were fed to small children to help them sleep more soundly. The field poppy is the most common variety, and is generally found on cultivated ground such as wheat fields, where the soil has been disturbed. They are the flowers that stain the fields of the countryside and brighten our verges. The wild poppy has been under threat from modern farming techniques, and the widespread use of herbicides still poses a threat to these cheerful flowers.

Origin From Europe to Asia.

Description This popular flower is probably one of the most readily recognized of around fifty species of annuals and perennials that are commonly referred to as poppies.

Colours Traditionally, red is the colour of poppies, but the range of colours is actually huge. *Papaver nudicaule* is available in all shades of orange, yellow, salmon, and white. The most popular colours for *P. orientale* and *P. somniferum* are red, pink, coral, and burgundy, but because these are very fashionable flowers at present, many new varieties are being trialed each year. The Himalayan poppy (*Meconopsis*) is the most amazing blue colour, but I have only seen this sold as a cut flower in the flower market of Tokyo, Japan.

Varieties *P. nudicaule*, which is a perennial poppy and commonly known as the Arctic or Icelandic poppy, is one of the most popular species as a cut flower. It is heavily cultivated in Italy around San Remo and in California in the USA. The main supply for this poppy is over the winter months and into summer. The cultivars 'Goodwin's Victory' and 'San Remo' are two of the most widely available. *P. orientale* – or the oriental poppy as it is commonly known – is sold seasonally in a range of colours. So, too, is *P. somniferum*, commonly known as the opium poppy. The attractive green seed heads from both these species are available over a much longer season. *P. somniferum* 'Hen and Chicken' is cultivated widely for its green seed pod.

Vase life Sadly, most poppies are short-lived, both in their natural habitat and also as cut flowers. *P. nudicaule* lasts between six and nine days. Most poppies are supplied with their stems singed because they exude a milky sap. If you need to trim the stems, it is essential that you re-singe them with a naked flame. The oriental and *somniferum* varieties generally last for only four to seven days, but they are in any case more useful to the florist for their seed heads. By the time the green seed head has developed, the stem is much stronger and will not need to be singed. These green seed heads can last for as long as four weeks.

Scent Slightly fragrant.

Use Today poppies are very fashionable both as garden plants and as cut flowers. The red poppy has been associated with war remembrance since the Greek poet Homer linked a hanging poppy bud with a dying soldier. *P. somniferum* 'Hen and Chicken' is cultivated widely for its seed pod – formed from one large seed head surrounded by smaller ones. Its very contorted form makes a useful addition to architectural arrangements or to massed and textural work.

Paphiopedilum

Common name Slipper orchid.

Origin Asia.

Description There is a huge amount of diversity within the genus; some slipper orchids are terrestrial, growing through the forest floor; others are lithophytes, which show a preference for limestone caves; while others live as epiphytes, hanging from trees in the rain forest. These flowers have long been highly prized in horticulture for their distinctive labellum or "pouch". They are cultivated throughout the world and new forms are discovered or created each year.

Colours Slipper orchids come in a huge range of colours, and many have fascinating markings. Some have plain leaves, while others have distinctive mottled foliage, which makes them attractive even without their flowers.

Varieties More than 20,000 varieties have been registered, and numerous new varieties are becoming available each year.

Vase life Four to six weeks as a cut flower. Slipper orchids have hairy stems that do not like being in deep water, so place in shallow water.

Scent None.

Use These long-lasting blooms are expensive and so their use tends to be restricted to specialist floristry for weddings and high-design work. They are so beautiful that they look best arranged on their own in individual specimen vases, with several of these grouped together. Mysterious and decadent, these are very treasured blooms.

Paphiopedilum hybrid 'Mitylene'

Phalaenopsis

Common name Moth orchid.

Origin Asia.

Description A single stem of loose clusters of flowers rises from leathery wide leaves at the base of the plant. The shiny dark leaves and silvery aerial roots are sometimes used in cut-flower arrangements.

Colours A great variety in colours and markings. White is by far the most popular both as a cut flower and as a pot plant, but there are also many variations of pink, purple, red, lilac, green, orange, and gold.

Varieties Phalaenopsis orchids are the most important orchids commercially: seven million plants are sold each year through the Dutch international auctions. They are generally marketed by colour, but the most popular white varieties for weddings are 'Cottonwood', 'Oregon', 'Delight', 'Snow City', and 'Taisuco'. A lot of the new hybrids have been smaller-headed and often rather unusual or brightly coloured. Such novelties have increased interest in this orchid. The more common white and pink varieties have lost some of their exclusivity, but these exotic beauties can now be enjoyed by a much larger public.

Vase life Two to three weeks. These orchids are usually sold in water phials and their stems should be recut and placed in deep water. Refresh flaccid flowers by submerging them in lukewarm water.

Scent None.

Uses Good for wedding bouquets, displaying in single vases, and in decorative floristry, these orchids are also excellent as pot plants.

Phalaenopsis 'Antique Gold'

Physalis alkekengi

Physalis

Common name Chinese lantern. *Physalis* means "water blister" and refers to the swollen fruit calyx.

Origin Japan.

Description Perennial, cultivated outdoors and growing to approximately 20in (50cm). It has a creeping rhizome, lightly haired stalks, and light green oval leaves with winged lead stalks. It is not the small white flowers that are of most interest to the flower arranger, however, but the puffed-out sepals of 2½–3in (6–8cm), which surround the berry.

Colours Orange sepal and berries.

Varieties *Physalis alkekengi* var. *franchetii* has larger decorative lanterns than other forms.

Vase life ten days or more, but the orange lanterns dry very well and can last in permanent decorations for up to two years.

Scent None.

Use Popular for autumn arrangements, particularly for harvest festivals or at Hallowe'en, when the orange flower is in season and the colour suits the time of year. The orange lanterns also make very cheerful dried flowers – they can easily be air-dried and will keep their bright colour very well. The seed heads can be wired into interesting designs and the flowers last reasonably well in water, making this a suitable flower for contract vases, either massed on its own or with other seasonal flowers. The linear form of the flowers makes them appropriate for vases and large arrangements.

*Native South African flowers with succulent cordata leaves and proteas (*Protea cynaroides *and P. nerifolia*) *mixed with cape foliage (*Leucadendron platysperum, L. coniferum, *and* Berzelia abrotanoides), *ornamental pineapples (*Ananas bracteatus*) and spiral gingers (*Costus spicatus*), with bun moss (*Leucobryum glaucum*) to fill in any gaps.*

Protea

Common name Collectively known as proteas, but individual varieties have their own common names.

Origin Originally from Australia and Africa, these exotic, unusual flowers are now widely cultivated in hot, arid climates all over the world, particularly America and Israel.

Description The family Proteaceae contains more than sixty genera and 1400 species. Proteas are woody plants cultivated outdoors. The shape of the flower is irregular, with four perianth segments that are also considered to be the sepals and which grow in alternation with the perianth petals. Some of the flowers are arched inward and the centre is double and surrounded by silken-haired bracts.

Colours Light pink, pinkish red, green, and white.

Varieties There are several different varieties that appear on the market at particular times of the year. There are also many different grades: as with most flowers, you tend to get what you pay for. *Protea compacta* is arched inward and is reddish pink. *P. grandiceps* is also pinky red and has a white centre and huge grey-green leaves. One of my personal favourites is *P. neriifolia*, which can be white, pinky red, or red, but is edged with purplish black, making it one of the most dramatic of the regular-sized varieties. Most interesting is the white *neriifolia*, which has an intriguing coloration of silver, grey, and green. The *repens* proteas all tend to have more outwardly facing petals and are more spiky. There are white, red, and pale pink varieties, which are normally sold by colour rather than specific name. Large varieties are found in the *P. magnifica* species and include 'Lady Di', 'Susara', 'Botriver Barbigera' and 'Sederberg Barbigera'. These are commonly known as the giant woolly-beard varieties, which describes them very accurately! Indisputably at the top of the range are the King proteas or Giant honey pots, *Protea cynaroides*. These giant-headed flowers are around 8in (20cm) in diameter and have thick leathery stalks. There are also some smaller varieties, which are sold in branches, including the grey-green *P. scolymocephala* and the red *P. pityphylla*.

Vase Cut off at least 1in (2.5cm) of the woody stem with secateurs and place in fairly deep water. Thoroughly clean any buckets with a proprietary cleaning fluid or bleach and do not pack the flowers in too tightly, as leaf blackening can be a problem with proteas. This is caused by the considerable heat that the flowers generate and particularly affects *P. repens*, *P. compacta*, *P. neriifolia*, and *P. magnifica*. Provide the flowers with good air circulation, ensure that the buckets are spotlessly clean, and keep the temperature low in order to prevent the problem occurring. Make sure, too, that there is no lower foliage in the water. As you will discover if you are using a clear glass vase, proteas can soon discolour the water, so change it frequently and add flower food. If the proteas are of top quality, and you look after them well, you will get a month of pleasure from these long-lasting beauties.

Scent None.

Use Proteas add colour, texture, and an architectural quality to floral arrangements. Thanks to their spectacular appearance and longevity, they are great plants for contract work. The giant King protea (*P. cynaroides*) looks fabulous arranged on its own with the occasional tropical leaf such as a monstera. I also love to arrange the pink protea with *Leucadendron argenteum* (Silver tree). Proteas also dry very well and so are suitable for more permanent displays.

Protea repens 'White Repens'

Protea cynaroides 'King'

Ranunculus asiaticus 'Fiandine'

Ranunculus

Common name Persian buttercup.

Origin From the eastern Mediterranean to Iran.

Description Tuberous plant growing to about 6–10in (15–25cm) tall, with beautiful peony-shaped flowers that are my all-time favourites. They have hairy stems and lower leaves that are ovate and trilobate, while upper ones are singly or doubly ternate with ovate, toothed segments.

Colours Various colours, from pastel pink, lemons, and apricots through to vivid reds, hot pink, deep burgundy, and brown, as well as lots of new speckled and spotted varieties, which are really gorgeous.

Varieties 'Ranobelle' and 'Pauline' are the most widely available as cut flowers and they are usually marketed by colour. The 'Ranobelle' variety includes dark yellow, dark pink, carmine, light yellow, light pink, orange, red, white, and salmon colour forms. The cappuccino spotted varieties are known as 'Picotee' and these also come in yellow, pink, and white. Two of my favourites are 'Pauline Violet' and 'Pauline Brown', which have the most exquisite deep colours: the violet is almost the colour of beetroot, while the brown is the colour of a good milk chocolate.

Vase life Eight to fourteen days. These beautiful flowers look their best the day before they expire, when their petals become translucent. Remove any lower foliage from the stems as they will contaminate the water.

Scent None.

Use Bouquets, bridal work, and arrangements. Grouped simply en masse in a vase they are sure to lift the spirits.

Ranunculus 'Ranobelle Inra Picotee Wit'

Ranunculus 'Ranobelle Inra Zalm'

Ranunculus 'Ranobelle Inra Lichtroze'

Rosa 'Ruby Red'

Rosa

Common name Rose.

Origin Present-day roses have a number of ancestors, some from India, some from China, and some that are native to Europe. Roses are the most frequently traded of all cut flowers.

Description There is a huge number of different species, but the commercially grown florists' flower is grown on stems of 8–39in (20cm–1m). The stems are always leafy and usually thorny.

Colours An astonishing range of colours and bicolours.

Varieties It is almost impossible to keep up with the names of florists' roses produced in the last five years – new varieties are appearing daily. There are four main categories: small-flowered, medium-flowered, large-flowered, and spray roses. Some of the most important recent varieties have been the 'Black Bacarra', which has burgundy-black petals; 'Circus', which is a bicolour yellow and orange; the peach 'Toscanini'; purple-pink 'Milano'; and the bicolour pink and cream 'Cézanne'.

Vase life Commercially grown roses for the cut-flower industry should last from eight to eighteen days, depending on the temperature and the cultivar; garden roses may last only three to seven days. Flower growers are continually crossing varieties that have a good vase life to produce stronger and better roses. Some of the new varieties are also thornless.

Scent Commercially-grown roses generally have no scent.

Use All areas of floristry and flower arranging. The wide variation in colour and size make roses the most popular flower in the industry.

Rosa 'Ambiance'

Rosa 'Nicole'

Rosa 'Handel'

Stephanotis floribunda

Stephanotis floribunda

Common name Madagascan jasmine.

Origin Madagascar.

Description Evergreen climbing shrub, cultivated in the hothouse, that has tendrils stretching for many feet and shiny, dark green, leathery leaves of 1–3in (2–8cm). The round axillary flower cluster grows on a short stalk. Flowers are approximately 1–1½in (2–4cm) long and have patulous lobes.

Colours White.

Varieties None.

Vase life Limited life span of three to five days as a cut flower. It can be bought as a houseplant and stored this way until the flower heads are required. The flowers are usually sold in bags or small boxes without any greenery, so if you want to use the green tendrils and vines, you will need to order this jasmine in plant form.

Scent Glorious scent.

Use This sturdy vine lives well as a houseplant in conservatories and glasshouses, but is also prized by florists, notably for its scent – it is a keynote scent for many perfumes. It is popular with brides all over the world, but particularly in the USA. Individually wired florets look great in headdresses, or simply wired into hair, and a mass of them makes a stunning bridal posy. A few heads floating in shallow dish of water, or added to a bowl of fruit, will make a simple table centrepiece, and I have also wound vines with flowers around napkins.

Symphoricarpos x *doorenbosii* 'Red Pearl'

Symphoricarpos

Common name Snowberry.

Origin Eastern Canada and the northern USA.

Description A broad bush with many runners and bare twigs. The leaves are 1½–3in (4–8cm) long, bluntly oval, often lobed, and have very short stalks. The pink flowers are grouped in dense bunches, but it is for its fruit that this plant is grown in the commercial cut-flower market. The ½in (12mm) berries are white or pink and are available from late summer until early winter. The branches are arched.

Colours White and pink berries.

Varieties Pink-berried varieties include 'Marleen', 'Mother of Pearl', 'Pink Pearl', 'Scarlet Pearl', and 'Red Pearl'. The most commonly available white-fruited varieties include 'White Hedge', 'White Pearl', and 'Gonny'.

Vase life Change the water frequently and the berries should last for up to two weeks; they will start to turn brown toward the end of this period. Vase life shortens later in the season.

Scent None.

Use The arched branches are very attractive in vases or arrangements.

Trachelium caeruleum

Common name Throatwort; *Trachelis* comes from the Greek, meaning throat. The plant was once used for medicinal purposes for throat and head ailments, and is still in parts of its native Balkans.

Origin The Balkans.

Description A perennial plant but, because it is not frost hardy, generally cultivated as an annual. The bright green leaves are nettle-like and oval with a pointed tip. The flower stem, often more than 2½ft (80cm) long, bears an umbel with a large number of small, bell-shaped flowers.

Colours The original colour was lilac, but the choice has now been extended to many shades of lilac, purple, and white, and some pinks.

Varieties For white varieties, look out for 'Lake Powell', 'Jemmy Wit', 'Album', and 'Helios'. For a rosier pink trachelium, try 'Corine Red', which appears occasionally throughout the year.

Vase life Eight to twelve days.

Scent None.

Use Tracheliums are available all year round and are very useful purple flowers as fillers in vases and large arrangements, particularly as they have quite long stems. They also work well massed low in arrangements and their large heads make them good value. I am a big fan of the white varieties, which look limey green and help to make the colour scheme of an arrangement appear livelier and fresher. However, white varieties can mark easily if they get damp in transit, so they are a bit less reliable than the dependable lilac and purple forms.

Delphiniums, both hybrid and belladonna, in my opinion look at their best when arranged with other seasonal flowers such as burgundy stocks (Matthiola incana), white trachelium (Trachelium caeruleum 'Album') and lilac lisianthus (Eustoma russellianum 'Misty Blue'). These colours are complemented by the lime green spires of bells of Ireland (Molucella laevis).

Tulipa 'Aladdin'

Tulipa

Common name Tulip.

Origin The north Himalayas. The Turks were the first real enthusiasts, but it was not until the 1550s that tulips reached the West.

Description Bulbous annual with a few wide, rather long leaves and one stalk, 10–16in (25–40cm) long, which – in nearly all cases – has a single flower. The flower comprises two crowns of three perianth leaves, two whirls of three stamens, and one pistil.

Colours An amazing variety. According to the Dutch, who grow 750 million tulips a year and supply most of the world market, yellow is the most popular colour.

Varieties The double yellow 'Monte Carlo' accounts for ten per cent of all tulips sold; the red 'Prominence' is another big player in the world tulip market. 'Lustige Witwe' and 'White Dream' are commonly available white varieties, while 'Christmas Marvel' and 'Angélique' (below left) are popular pink ones. Parrot tulips include 'Salmon Parrot' and 'Black Parrot' (below); fringed ones the red 'Arma', yellow 'Hamilton', and purple 'Corridor'. Lily-flowering tulips are more pointed; popular ones are 'Aladdin' (left), orangey red 'Royal Design', and the orange 'Ballerina'.

Vase life Tulips do not need any special conditioning, but do remember that they will often continue to grow in water, sometimes by as much as 2in (5cm). They should last between five and ten days.

Scent None.

Use Good for hand-tied bouquets and vases (in water not foam).

Tulipa 'Angélique'

Tulipa 'Black Parrot'

Tulips arranged in groups of colours in a blue glass vase designed by the architect Alva Aalto. Many varieties of flowers are now artificially dyed to increase sales. Here 'White Dream' tulips have drunk blue dye to give them a blue tinge. They are mixed with two popular yellow tulips – the pointed 'Yokohama' and the fringed 'Royal Sphinx' – and the lily-flowering 'Aladdin'.

Vanda

Vanda

Common name Vanda orchid.

Origin The national flower of Singapore has recently started appearing in large quantities as a cut flower.

Description This orchid is an epiphyte, meaning that it grows on the branches of other plants.

Colours With their exotic shape and vibrant colour, vanda orchids have been an instant hit. Purple is the most popular and widely available colour, but bright pink vandas are also becoming more common.

Varieties There are approximately eighty vanda varieties, but at present these orchids are sold as cut flowers by colour rather than by variety.

Vase life This flower may be expensive to buy, but it lasts an impressive three weeks in water and so gives excellent value. Change the water weekly, and if the flowers become limp, submerge them in lukewarm water until they revive. If using vanda orchids in florist's foam, place them in water phials first and insert these into the foam so that the flowers receive plenty of water.

Scent None.

Use Perfect for buttonholes, corsages, and exotic arrangements, vandas are also good for contract work because of their longevity. The vanda flower is offered as a gift in its native Singapore, and is also often used in Hawaiian garlands as a symbol of hospitality and welcome.

Zantedeschia aethiopica 'Colombe de Paix'

Zantedeschia

Common name Calla or arum lily.

Origin Africa, where it grows wild and its warmed leaves are still used as a natural cure for headaches or pain relief from insect bites.

Description Herbaceous perennial with large arrow-shaped leaves. The fleshy stalk, usually 2–3ft (60–90cm) long, has a funnel-shaped bract, known as a spathe, which has a flat margin. The flowering spadix and the spathe surrounding it are the same length.

Colours With an increasing number of eye-catching colours in a range of muted and bright shades, this flower is sought after all year round. White is the most common colour, but others include variations on yellow, burgundy, pink, orange, red, purple, and black.

Varieties The popularity of calla lilies has led to the development of a range of smaller-flowering varieties in many different colours, including 'Florex Gold', 'Pink Persuasion', 'Apricot Glow', and 'Chianti'. For one of the darkest callas, look out for the almost black 'Schwarzwalder'.

Vase life Recut stems diagonally and give them a good drink before arranging these lilies in florist's foam. Change the water at least every three days if they are arranged in a vase. You can protect the stems from splitting by taping the ends with clear tape. If looked after well, calla lilies should last three weeks.

Scent None.

Use These are very versatile flowers, which are useful for all aspects of floristry and flower arranging.

Zantedeschia aethiopica 'Green Goddess'

Zantedeschia 'Mango'

Index of botanical names

Page references in *italics* refer to illustrations.

A

Acacia 86, 87
Achillea 76, 77
    A. filipendulina: 'Cream Perfection' 48;
    'Moonshine' *193*
    A. millefolium: 'Inca Gold' *27*;
    'Martina' 82
    A. 'Paprika' 86
Aconitum 13, 71
Aesculus hippocastanum 134
Agapanthus 71, 86, 87
    A. africanus 42, *43*
Alchemilla mollis 56, 74, 84, 122, 126, 144
Allium 15
    A. ampeloprasum 7
    A. giganteum 42
    A. sphaerocephalon 199
Alpinia purpurata 26, 189
Amaranthus 88
    A. caudatus 76, 77; 'Albiflora' 154;
    'Green Tails' 50
    A. hypochondriacus 46, 47; 'Pigmy Viridis'
    52, 53; 'Viridis' 40, 41
Ananas
    A. bracteatus 222
    A. comosus 84
Anemone 86, 105, 177, 178
    A. coronaria 186; 'Galil' 186; 'Marianne'
    186; 'Marianne Blue' *185*; 'Marianne
    Red' 160; 'Mona Lisa' 186, *187*; 'Mona
    Lisa Orchid' *186*; 'Mona Lisa White'
    20, 186
    A. japonica 213
Anethum
    A. graveolens 7, 14, 40, 48, 50, 64, 68,
    71, 76, 86, 105, 122, 170, 177, 187;
    'Lumina' 187; 'Mammoth' 187;
    'Vierling' 187
Angelica 14
Anthriscus sylvestris 14, 76
Anthurium
    A. andraeanum 15, 188, *193*; 'Acropolis'
    146; 'Amigo' 188; 'Baron' 146; 'Cheers'
    146, 188; 'Choco' 188; 'Cognac' 146,
    188; 'Fantasia' *188*; 'General' 146;
    'Greenpeace' 188; 'Laguna' 189; 'Midori'
    146, 188; 'Neon' 188; 'Rapido' 146, 188;
    'Safari' 188; 'Scarletta' 96; 'Simba' 46;
    'Sonate' *189*; 'Sultan' 146; 'Terra' 146,
    188; 'Tropical' 188; 'Vanilla' 188
Aquilegia 16
Arachnis 189
    'James Storei' 132, 189; 'Maggie Oei'
    52, 132, 189
Aranthera 'James Storei' see Arachnis
    'James Storei'
Arecastrum 189
Arundo donax 76
Asclepias
    'Cinderella' 92
    A. fruticosa *185*
    A. physocarpa 'Moby Dick' 138
    A. tuberosa 86; 'Beatrix' 56; 'Gay
    Butterfly' 50
Ascocentrum curvifolium 'Tang' 120

Aspidistra 185
Astilbe 64, 190
    'Diamant' 84, 190; 'Erika' 190;
    'Montgomery' 92; 'Visions' 190;
    'Wahsington' ('Washington') 190
Astrantia 76
    A. major 'Alba' 82
Avena
    A. fatua 40
    A. sativa 76

B

Banksia
    B. ashbeyi 60
    B. collina 26
Berberis 115
Berzelia
    B. abrotanoides 222
    B. galpinii 156
Betulus 90
Bouvardia
    'Arethusa' 190; 'Arthemy' 190;
    'Bridesmaid' 190; 'Caroline' 36; 'Daphne'
    190; 'Pink Luck' 190; 'President
    Cleveland' *190*; 'Royal Katy' 190
    B. leiantha 190
    B. longiflora 190
    B. ternifolia 190
Brassica 14
    B. bullata 154
    B. oleracea 191; 'Coblanc' 98; 'Corgy
    Dark Carmine' 152; 'Corgy Pink' 98,
    191; 'Corgy White' 191; 'Sunrise' 191;
    'Sunset' 191; 'White Crane' 191
Brassocattleya 192
Bupleurum
    B. griffithi 52
    B. griffithii *27*, 56

C

Calathea crotalifera 189
Calendula 86
    C. officinalis 28, 56
Callicarpa
    C. bodinieri 191; var. giraldii
    'Profusion' 191
Camellia 150, 152
    C. japonica 34
Campanula
    C. cochleariifolia 36
    C. medium 192
    C. medium 'Roze' *192*
    C. persicifolia 192
    C. pyramidalis 42, 192
Cannomis virgata 203
Capsicum frutescens 96, 115
Carex flacca 'Schreb' 40
Carthamus tinctorius 40, *179*
Castenea sativa 50
Cattleya walkeriana var. 'Alba' 192
Celosia 193
    'Bombay Yellow' 193; 'Century Paars'
    193; 'Cynthia Rose' 193; 'No 9' *193*;
    'Torch' 193
    C. argentia 'Bombay Pink' 156, *193*
Centaurea cyanus 105
Chrysanthemum 71, 128, 194
    'Dark Flamenco' 98; 'Delistar' 34;

'Dracula' *138*; 'Ellen Geel' *185*; 'Fred
Shoesmith' *16*; 'Gompie Geel' 98; 'Pizzy'
195; 'Purple Pennine Wine' 98; 'Reagan
White' *194*; 'Shamrock' 98, *194*; 'Tom
Pearce' 60, *194*
Cirsium 76
Clematis vitalba 16, 88, 136
    'Emerald Forest' 134
Codiaeum variegatum 112
Consolida 13
Convallaria majalis 12, 86, 105
Cordata 66
Cornus 118
    C. alba: 'Argenteo-Marginata' 138;
    'Aurea' 138; 'Elegantissima' 158;
    'Siberica' 138
Corylus avellana 'Contorta' 132, 166
Costus spicatus 222
Cotinus
    C. coggygria 126; 'Purpurea' 52; 'Royal
    Purple' 80, 100
Cotoneaster 100
Craspedia 15, 114
Crassula rupestris 38
Crocosmia 86, 88
    'Lucifer' 146
    C. aurea 'Emily McKenzie' 112
Cucurbita maxima 96, 98
Cyclamen 146
Cymbidium 80, 108, 196
    'Alice Anderson' *196*; 'Green Fantasy'
    140; 'Spring' *80*
Cynara 14
    C. cardunculus 170, 197
    C. scolymus 76, 197; 'Green Globe' 197;
    'Gros Vert de Leon' 197; 'Violetto
    Precoce' 197
Cypripedium 178, *179*

D

Dahlia 198
    'Arabian Nights' 90, 126, 198; 'Black
    Knight' 152; 'Black Pearl' 198; 'Charlie
    Kenwood' 126; 'Franz Kafka' 198;
    'Karma Fuchsiana' 126, 198; 'Karma
    Lagoon' 198; 'Karma Ohara' 198;
    'Karma Serena' 198; 'Molly Mooney'
    126; 'Night Queen' 198; 'Piper's Pink'
    126; 'Ruskin Dance' 126; 'Sarum
    Queen' *198*
Danäe racemosa 36
Dasylirion 114, 177, 180
Daucus carota 'Dara' 199
Delphinium 13, 15, 86, 200, 229
    'Cristel' *200*; 'Princess Caroline' 200;
    'White Arrow' 100, *200*; 'Yvonne'
    68, 100
    D. ajacis 200
    D. belladonna 'Volkerfieden' 168, 200
    D. consolida 86
    D. elatum: 'Alie Duyvensteyn' 120;
    'Harlecijn' 120, 199; 'Ned' 36
Dendrobium 'Tang' 110
Dianthus 128, 178, *179*, 201
    'Barbarella Purple' *201*; 'Cappuccino'
    162; 'Ceram' 156; 'Charmeur' 162;
    'Clove' 158, 162; 'Dark Pierrot' *154*,
    162; 'Doris' 72; 'Haytor' 72; 'Oliver' 162;

'Opale' 201; 'Pampa' *201*; 'Pierrot' 154;
'Prado' 128, 162; 'Prado Refit' 140;
'Rendez-Vous' *201*; 'Rosa Monica' *162*;
'Scia' 154, 162
D. barbatus 86, 201
D. caryophyllus 201

E

Echinops 15, 179
E. bannaticus 202; 'Blue Globe' *202*;
'Taplow Blue' 202
E. ritro 202; 'Veitch Blue' 202
Equisetum 21
E. giganteum 132
E. hyemale 40
Eremurus 42
Eryngium 202
E. alpinium 203
E. giganteum 202
E. planum 202; 'Blue Bell' 202; 'Blue
Ribbon' 202; 'Orion' 202; 'Supernova'
202; 'Tetra Petra' 202
Eucalyptus 88, 177
E. globulus 46
E. palanthemos 46
E. polyanthemos 36
Eucharis grandiflora 86
Eucomis bicolor 60, 162
Eugenia uniflora 115
Eupatorium 76
Euphorbia 76, 177
'Yellow River' 50
E. fulgens 86
Eustoma russellianum 13, 71, 86, 203
'Ballet Star' 168; 'Echo' 203; 'Fuji' 203;
'Kyoto Purple' 68; 'Mariachi' 203;
'Mariachi Pink' 71, 203; 'Misty Blue'
229; 'Piccolo' 203; 'Scirpus' 168

F

Fagus sylvatica purpurea 46, 76
Fatsia japonica 132
Foeniculum vulgare 86
Fragaria hybrids 72
Freesia 105, 179
Fritilleria
F. imperialis 86, 114
F. meleagris 114

G

Galanthus nivalis 'Flore Pleno' 32
Galax aphylla 48, 84, 92, 102, 152
Gaultheria shallon 38
Genista 48, 86
Gerbera 14, 24, 71, 179, 204
'Anais' *204*; 'Barcelona' 88; 'Bordeaux'
88; 'Cosmo' *204*; 'Doctor Who' *10*;
'Ferrari' *204*; 'Mystique' 152; 'Paso' *205*;
'Polka' *205*; 'Ruby Red' 150; 'Salsa' *205*;
'Tamara' 88; 'Tiramisu' 52; 'Whisper'
185
Gleichenia polypodiodes 26
Gloriosa 18, 86, 205
G. superba: 'Citrina' 205; 'Grandiflora'
205; 'Rothschildiana' 122, 185, 205;
'Simplex' 205

H

Hamamelis mollis 210
Hardeum 40
Hebe
H. cupressoides 56; 'Boughton
Dome' 66
Hedera helix 42, 50, 54, 68, 88, 112, 130,
160, 178
Helianthus annuus 7, 20, 112, 206
'Flame' 170; 'Full Sun' 170; 'Italian
White' 206; 'Moonlight' *206*; 'Moulin
Rouge' 206; 'Orit' 206; 'Prado Red' 170;
'Primrose' 206; 'Ring of Fire' 206; 'Ruby
Eclipse' 206; 'Snittgold' 206; 'Sonja' 206;
'Sunbright' 206; 'Sungold' 206; 'Sunrich
Lemon' 206; 'Sunrich Orange' 206;
'Teddy Bear' 50, 60, 120, *207*; 'Titan'
206; 'Vanilla Ice' 206
Helichrysum bracteatum 27
Heliconia 208
H. bihai 'Emerald Forest' 118
H. caribaea 208; 'Black Magic' 208;
'Gold' 208; 'Vermilion' *208*
H. chartacea 'Sexy Pink' *189*, 208
H. latispatha 'Gyro' *208*
H. psittacorum 208; 'Golden Torch' 208;
'Parrot' 136; 'Suriname Sassy' 208
H. rastrata 'Ruiz and Pavon' *208*
H. stricta 208; 'Firebird' 22
Helixine soleirolii 168
Helleborus niger 15, 48
Hermodactylus tuberosa 27, 210, 211
Hippeastrum 18, 42, 86, 178, 209
'Ambiance' 209; 'Apple Blossom' *19*,
209; 'Christmas Gift' 209; 'Hercules'
209; 'Liberty' 209; 'Ludwig Dazzler' *209*;
'Minerva' 209; 'Mont Blanc' 209;
'Nymph' 209; 'Red Lion' 209; 'Rilona'
209; 'Roma' 209; 'Royal Velvet' 209;
'Telstar' *11*
H. gracilis 'Pygmee' 209
Hippophäe rhamnoides 115
Hosta 203
'August Moon' 76
Hyacinthoides campanulatus 105
Hyacinthus 86, 179
Hydrangea 80, 210
H. macrophylla 27, 42, 112, 210; 'Blue
Tit' 100; 'Green Shadow' 34
H. paniculata 201
Hypericum 66, 88
'Autumn Blaze' 96; 'Jade' 80

I

Ilex aquifolium 160
Iris 14, 18, 211
'Apollo' 27; 'Black' *211*; 'Blue Diamond'
211; 'Blue Magic' *210*, 211; 'Golden
Harvest' 211; 'Hong Kong' 211; 'Ideal'
210, 211; 'Professor Blaauw' 211;
'White Wedgwood' 211; 'Yellow
Queen' 211
Ixia 'Spotlight' 48

K

Kniphofia 'Royal Standard' 52

L

Lachenalia 'Quadricolour' 27
Lagurus ovatus 40
Larix 86
Lathyrus 212
L. latifolius 105, 212
L. odoratus 12, 84, 92, 102, 212; 'Jayne
Amanda' *212*; 'Noel Sutton' 212;
'White Supreme *84*
Laurus nobilis 162
Lavandula 80, 105
Leucadendron
'Flora Bush' 156; 'Safari Sunset' 7, 132
L. coniferum 222
L. discolor 132
L. laureolum 132
L. platysperum 222
Leucobryum glaucum 114, 222
Leucospermum 213
'African Red' 213; 'Fire Dance' 213;
'Flamespike' 213; 'High Gold' 213;
'Yellow Bird' 213
L. conocarpodendron 213
L. cordifolium 152, 213; 'Green' 156;
'Red Sunset' 26, 156; 'Sunrise' 156, 213;
'Tango' *152*; 'Vlam' *213*
L. erubescens 213
L. leutens 88
L. patersonii 213
L. tottum 'Scarlet Ribbon' 213
Ligature vulgare 80
Ligustrum 42, 88, 100, 152, *185*
L. japonicum 154
L. obtusifolium 'Aurea Marginata' 160
Lilium 71, 177, 214
'Acapulco' 214; 'Alaska' 214; 'Avignon'
214; 'Casablanca' 36, 42, 214; 'Chianti'
214; 'Connecticut King' 214; 'Côte
d'Azur' 214; 'Dolce Vita' *214*; 'Golden
Splendour' 50; 'Imperial Gold' 82; 'La
Rêve' *214*; 'Medusa' 68; 'Mero Star' 214;
'Monte Negro' 214; 'Romanesco' 68;
'Sorbonne' 214; 'White Europe' 214
L. regale 64
Limonium suworowii 213
Litchi chinensis 27, 115
Lonicera periclymenum 'Serotina' 22
Lupinus 76
Lycospericum 96
Lysimachia 76

M

Malus 215
'Bob White' 215; 'Butterball' 215;
'Harvest Gold' 215; 'Professor
Sprenger' 215; 'Red Jewell' 215; 'Red
Peacock' 215; 'Red Sentinel' 50, 136,
215; 'Wintergold' 215
M. domestica 'Crimson King' 136
Malva 76
Matthiola 76, 86
M. incana 229
Meconopsis 220
Millum 76
Miscanthus sinensis 'Zebrinus' 60
Mokkara
'Mok' 189; 'Patou Siam' 189; 'Robin'
189; 'Ruby' 189; 'Tangerine' 189;

'Tangerine Tang' 132
Moluccella laevis 13, 68, 71, 203, 229
Musa 94
    M. ornata 132
Muscari 12, 102
    M. armeniacum 154
Myrica gale 210
Mysotis 12, 86, 102

N
Narcissus 86, 216
    'Bridal Crown' 102; 'Carlton' 216;
    'Charity May' 27; 'Cheerfulness' 216;
    'Dick Wilden' 216; 'Dutch Master' 216;
    'Geranium' 216; 'Golden Ducat' 27,
    216; 'Golden Harvest' 216; 'Ice Follies'
    216; 'Jumblie' 86; 'Liberty Bells' 48;
    'Paper White' 102, 216; 'Soleil d'Or'
    216; 'Suzy' 216; 'Tahiti' 216; 'Yellow Sun'
    216; 'Ziva' 217
Nelumbo nucifera 185, 193
Nepenthes maxima 18
Nerine 18, 71
    N. bowdenii: 'Corusca Major' 19, 96,
    120; 'Lady Cynthia' 140
Nigella damascena 82, 92

O
Oncidium 12
    O. 'Golden Shower' 218
Origanum 76
    O. vulgare 'Purple beauty' 199
Ornithogalum
    O. arabicum 66, 203
    O. thyrsoides 105

P
Pandanus odoratissimus 60
Panicum vergatum 'Fountain' 34
Pæonia 71, 86, 219
    'Bowl of Beauty' 219; 'Charlie's White'
    74; 'China Rose' 74, 218; 'Coral Charm'
    219; 'Dr Alexander Fleming' 219;
    'Duchesse de Nemours' 74, 218, 219;
    'Festiva Maxima' 219; 'Gardenia' 36, 74;
    'Karl Rosenfield' 74, 219; 'Knighthood'
    218; 'Lady Alexandra Duff' 74;
    'Monsieur Jules Elie' 74; 'Pink Panther'
    219; 'Red Charm' 219; 'Sarah
    Bernhardt' 74, 185, 218, 219; 'Shirley
    Temple' 74, 218, 219
Papaver 15, 76, 199, 203, 220
    P. nudicaule 17, 220; 'Goodwin's Victory'
    220; 'San Remo' 220
    P. orientale 40, 220; 'Allegro Viva' 220
    P. somniferum 220; 'Hen and
    Chicken' 220
Paphiopedilum 15, 221
    'Mytilene' 221
Passiflora 15
Pennisetum setaceum 40
Penstemon 'Peace' 213
Phalaenopsis 108, 221
    'Antique Gold' 221; 'Cottonwood' 221;
    'Delight' 221; 'Oregon' 221; 'Snow City'
    221; 'Taisuco' 221
Philadelphus coronarius 76
Phlomis 76

Phoenix roebelenii 42, 189
Phormium 118
    P. tenax 150; 'Variegatum' 60
Photinia x fraseri 'Red Robin' 60
Physalis 27, 115, 222
    P. alkengi var. *franchetii* 222
Pittosporum tenuifolium 46
Primula 86
    P. vulgaris 48, 105
Protea 223
    P. compacta 223
    P. cynaroides 26, 222, 223; 'King' 223
    P. grandiceps 26, 223
    P. magnifica 223; 'Botriver Barbigera'
    223; 'Lady Di' 223; 'Sederberg
    Barbigera' 223; 'Susara' 223
    P. neriifolia 222, 223
    P. pityphylla 223
    P. repens 60, 223; 'White Repens' 223
    P. scolymocephala 223
Prunus
    P. avium 115
P. glandulosa 'Alba Plena' 210

Q
Quercus 96
    Q. ellipsoidalis 50

R
Ranunculus 21, 86, 224
    'Apricot' 56; 'Pauline' 224; 'Pauline
    Brown' 224; 'Pauline Violet' 224;
    'Picotee' 224; 'Ranobelle' 224;
    'Ranobelle Inra Lichtroze' 225;
    'Ranobelle Inra Picotee Wit' 224;
    'Ranobelle Inra White' 32;
    'Ranobelle Inra Zalm' 224
    R. asiaticus 'Fiandine' 224
Rosa 12, 54, 71, 105, 130, 199, 226
    'Aalsmeer Gold' 90; 'Ambiance' 58,
    226; 'Aqua' 80, 94, 148, 164;
    'Aretha' 150; 'Athena' 58; 'Black
    Bacarra' 58, 82, 160, 164, 226;
    'Black Beauty' 84; 'Black Magic' 7;
    'Blanca' 36; 'Blue Moon' 86;
    'Candy Bianca' 142; 'Cézanne' 226;
    'Champagne' 82; 'Cherry Lady' 120;
    'Circus' 226; 'Confetti' 90, 94;
    'Coolwater' 148, 164; 'Diplomat' 68;
    'Eden' 34, 68; 'Grand Prix' 58, 150, 164;
    'Handel' 227; 'Heaven' 144; 'Illusion' 19,
    144; 'Lemon and lime' 58; 'Leonardis'
    64, 66; 'Metallica' 142, 144; 'Milano' 80,
    126, 185, 226; 'Milva' 58; 'Naranga' 126,
    152; 'Nicole' 86, 90, 94, 150, 226;
    'Nicole Pink' 193; 'Peer Gynt' 64;
    'Pretty Woman' 122, 164; 'Ruby Red'
    19, 124, 150, 226; 'Sphinx' 58, 112;
    'Stirling Silver' 86; 'Tamango' 94;
    'Toscanini' 226; 'Tressor 2000' 120, 122;
    'Vendelle' 38, 144; 'Versillea' 66; 'Vicky
    Brown' 86; 'Wow' 185; 'Xtreme' 92,
    142, 144, 164; 'Yellow Success' 100
    R. canina 96, 100, 126, 152
    R. micro ' Lemon' 48
Rosemarinus officinalis 80, 86, 105
Rudbeckia 64, 66, 170
    R. hirta 52

Rumex 76
Ruta graveolens 76
    'Jackman's Blue' 72

S
Salix 177
    S. caprea 86
    S. matsudana 'Tortuosa' 170
Salvia 105
Saponaria 76
Scabiosa 76
Scirpus tabernaemontani 'Zebrinus' 118
Sedum spectabile 13, 34, 80
Senecio greyii 64, 80, 126
Skimmia japonica
    'Rubella' 66, 160; 'Rubinetta' 152
Sorbus aria 'Lutescens' 46, 86
Sphagnum auriculatum 46, 134, 160
Spiraea x vanhouttei 'Bridal Wreath' 46
Stephanotis floribunda 104, 105, 228
Strelitzia reginae 23, 152
Symphoricarpos 228
    'Gonny' 228; 'Marleen' 228; 'Mother
    of Pearl' 228; 'Pink Pearl' 34, 68, 80,
    142, 228; 'Red Pearl' 34, 228; 'Scarlet
    Pearl' 228; 'White Hedge' 228;
    'White Pearl' 228
    S. albus 42
Syringa 86

T
Tanacetum
    T. vulgare 105, 126; 'Isle Gold' 52
Telopea speciosissima 26
Thamnochortus insignis 205
Tillandsia usneoides 134
Trachelium
    'Album' 229; 'Corine Red' 229;
    'Helios' 36, 229; 'Jemmy Wit' 229;
    'Lake Powell' 229
    T. caeruleum 229; 'Lake Superior' 152
Trillium 15
Triticum aestivum 40
Tulipa 105
    'Aladdin' 230, 231; 'Angélique' 230;
    'Arma' 230; 'Ballerina' 230; 'Black
    Parrot' 230; 'Christmas Marvel' 229;
    'Corridor' 230; 'Fancy Frill' 102; 'Flaming
    Parrot' 86; 'Hamilton' 230; 'Lustige
    Witwe' 230; 'Madison Garden' 205;
    'Monte Carlo' 230; 'Prominence' 230;
    'Royal Design' 230; 'Royal Sphinx' 231;
    'Salmon Parrot' 230; 'White Dream'
    230, 231; 'Yokohama' 231
Typha latifolia 96

V
Vaccinium 115
Valeriana 76
Vanda 25, 108, 231
    V. rothschildiana 166
Verbascum 76
Veronica 213
Viburnum 64
    V. lantana 68
    V. opulus 32, 52, 86, 88, 210
    V. tinus 126, 138
Vinca major 105

General index

Viola 15
   V. odorata 105
   V. wittrockiana 15
Vitis quinquefolia 88

X

Xanthorrhoea
   X. preissii 162; 'Black Boy' 60
Xerophyllum
   X. asphodeloides 48, 158
   X. tenax 27

Y

Yucca aloifolia 118, 170

Z

Zantedeschia 14, 232
   'Apricot Glow' *232*; 'Chianti' 156,
   232; 'Florex Gold' 52, 110,
   232; 'Golden Affair' 62;
   'Little Dream' 62; 'Little Jim' 62;
   'Majestic Red' *193*; 'Mango' 62,
   232; 'Pink Persuasion' 62, 232, *233*;
   'Schwarzwalder' 232;
   'Yellow Queen' 62
   Z. aethiopica 42; 'Colombe
   de Paix' *232*; 'Green Goddess'
   232; 'Highwood' *203*;
   'Tinkerbell' 42
Zingiber zerumbet 7

Page references in *italics* refer to
illustrations. Cross references to
Latin-based names refer to the index
of botanical names.

A

Aalto, Alvar *231*
African lily see *Agapanthus africanus*
African thatchreed see
   Thamnochortus insignis
Amaryllis see *Hippeastrum*
Arabian chincherinchee see
   Ornithogalum arabicum
arrangement styles
   asymmetrical 16, 26
   cascade *18*, 174
   circular 26, 32–3, 52–3, 66–7, 92–3,
   100–1, 110–11, 162–3
   linear 26, 136, *137*
   natural 26, 27, 40–1, 46–7, 130–1
   parallel 26
   round see circular above
   symmetrical 16, 26, 132–3
   textured 156–7, 222
   topiary see topiary arrangements
   vegetative see natural above
arrangements
   for Christmas 34, 138–9, 142, 160–1
   classic 30–105
   "contained" 29, 108–9, 114–17, 148–9
   contemporary 106–71
   Dutch "Old Master" style 86–7
   hand-tied 40–1, 62–3, 68–71, 92–3,
   177, 185, 213
   hanging 82–3, 100–1, 174
   for harvest suppers 88
   informal 74, 76–9, 213
   large 42–5
   for mantelpieces 50–1
   for Mothers' Day 102–3
   pedestal 42–5, 68–71
   for the table 12, 80–1 see *also*
   centrepieces
   for Thanksgiving 88
   trailing 50–1, 76–9, 88–9
   two-tiered 84–5, 205
   for weddings 34, 62, 108–9, 124,
   152–3, 196, 199
   see *also* arrangement styles
artichoke 14
arum lily see *Zantedeschia aethiopica*
Asian floristry 24

B

balance 56, 62
banana see *Musa*
barberry see *Berberis*
barley see *Hardeum*
baubles see *Berzelia galpinii*
bead vine see *Crassula rupestris*
bear grass see *Dasylirion*; *Xerophyllum
   asphodeloides*; *Xerophyllum tenax*
beauty berry see *Callicarpa bodinieri*
bells of Ireland see *Moluccella laevis*
berries 52, 96, 112, 126, 152, 154, 191
   ivy 28, 80, 82, 122, 128, 152, 210
birch see *Betulus*
bird of paradise see *Strelitzia reginae*

black cherry 84
bleach 114, 190, 225
blue gum eucalyptus see
   Eucalyptus globulus
bluebell see *Hyacinthoides campanulatus*
broom see *Genista*
buckets 44, 71, 76, 168
bullrush see *Typha latifolia*
bun moss see *Leucobryum glaucum*
Burgundy dill see *Daucus carota* 'Dara'

C

cabbage see *Brassica*
cacti 205
calla lily see *Zantedeschia aethiopica*
candelabra/candlesticks 82–3, 146–7, 174
candles 80–1, 82–3, 144–5
Canterbury bell see *Campanula*
Cape gooseberry see *Physalis*
cardoon see *Cynara cardunculus*
carnations 128, 162 see *also Dianthus*
catkins 16, 18
centrepieces 64–5, 80–1, 144–5, 160–1
Chatto, Beth 60
cherry see *Prunus avium*
chilli pepper see *Capsicum*
chimney bellflower see
   Campanula pyramidalis
chincherinchee see
   Ornithogalum thyrsoides
Chinese lantern see *Physalis*
Christmas rose see *Helleborus niger*
chrysanthemums 128 see *also
   Chrysanthemum*
cinnamon sticks 144–5
cock's comb see *Celosia*
colour 18, 36, 46, 52, 86, 110, 136, 142
Condor, Joseph 22
containers 28, 50, 76, 126, 210
   concealing
      with grass 21, 118–19
      with leaves 20, 21, 28, 48–9,
      80–1, 132–3
      cube vases 122–3, 138–9, 150–1
   decorating
      with flowers 122–3, 170–1
      with fruit 114–15
      with grass 80, 115, 158, 180
      with leaves 20, 94, 112–13, 150–1,
      162–3
      with twigs 138, 144, 210
   globes *29*, 114–17, 148–9, *193*
   grouping 24, 25
   Perspex 120–1, 164–5
   rubber 126–7
   test tubes 166–7
   urns 32–3, 42–5, 54–5, 68–71, 86–7,
   128–9, 168–9
   vegetables used 96–7, 154–5
   window boxes 50
   wire 46–7, 84–5, 168–9
   zinc *25*
copper beech see *Fagus sylvatica pupurea*
coral fern see *Gleichenia polypodiodes*
cornflower see *Centaurea cyanus*
cow parsley see *Anthriscus sylvestris*
crab apple see *Malus*
cranberry see *Vaccinium*

croton see *Codiaeum variegatum*
crown imperial see *Fritilleria imperialis*
cup and saucer plant see *Campanula*

D

date palm see *Phoenix roebelenii*
deconstructed designs 24, 25, 38–9, 164–5, 184
dill see *Anethum graveolens*
dock see *Rumex*
dogwood see *Cornus*
Dutch floristry 26

E

equipment 174, *175*
  candle cups 82, 174, *175*
  Cellophane/Cellocoup 8, 174, 180, *181*
  cocktail sticks 72
  cones 44, 174, *175*
  designer board 144
  dry-hard clay 174, *175*
  florist's fix 140, 152, 174, *175*
  florist's spike/frog 174, *175*
  florist's tie 71
  foam 46, 50, 54, 72, 100, 128, 174, 175
    balls 16, 58, 90, *175*, 189
    rings 65, 152, *175*
    sheets 144
  frames 27, 34, 134
  garden canes *24*, 44, 128, 174, *175*
  glue 20, 21, 38, 134
  glue guns 28, 38, 134, 144, 170
  hanging baskets 100, 174, *175*
  knives 94, 122, 174, *175*
  pew ends 174, *175*
  pin holders 11, 140, 152, 174, *175*
  pins 174, *175*, 178, *179*
  poles 16, 34, 90, 98, 189
  raffia 48, 84, 92, 118, 120, 174, 177, 180
  ribbon 84, 104, 174, *175*, 180, *181*
  rope 80, 174, *175*, 180
  scissors 174, *175*
  secateurs 174, *175*
  small-spray trays 174, *175*
  tape 124, 160, 174, *175*, 178
    double-sided 21, 28, 48, 80, 118, 162, 174, *175*
    wire-edged 158
  tubes 44
  vine bouquet holders 38
  wire 174, *175*, 178
    aluminium 108
    binding 178
    copper 138
    reel wire 134, 138, 174, 178
    rose wire *175*, 178
    silver wire 38, 174, *175*, 178
    stub wire 32, 174, *175*
  wire mesh 22, 44, 98, 100, 174, *175*
ethylene gas 28, 72
European floristry 18, 22, 24, 38, 138
everlasting pea see *Lathyrus latifolius*

F

feathers 124–5
fennel see *Foeniculum vulgare*
florist's spirea see *Astilbe*

flower food 18, 45, 160
flower shapes 18, 52
  bell 14
  branch 13
  composite 14, 16
  corymb 13
  globular 15, 16
  irregular 15, 16
  panicle 12
  raceme 15
  rosette 14, 16
  simple *14*, 15
  spike 13
  star 14, 20
  umbel 14, 18
  unusual 15
flowers
  buds 176
  buying 184
  conditioning 45, 76, 88, 100, 114
  decorating containers 122–3, 170–1
  dyed 231
  as fillers 13, 15, 44, 50, 52, 71
  for fragrance 36
  for hand-tying practice 40, 94, 158
  in paintings 40, 86, 136
  prolonging life 176
  shapes see flower shapes
  structure 12
  submerged 18, 22, 28, 29, 58–9, 108–9, 166–7, 193
  transporting 68, 180, *181*
  wrapping 180, *181*
Foley, Vivienne *19*
foliage 46–7, 65, 88, 96, 118, 152, 154
forget-me-not see *Myosotis*
fountain grass see *Panicum vergatum* 'Fountain'
foxtail lily see *Eremurus*
French hortensia see *Hydrangea*
fruit 84–5, 222
  submerged 28, 64–5, 114–17, 136–7
  in topiary arrangements 27, 72–3
  wiring 160–1, 178

G

gagel see *Myrica gale*
giant honey pot see *Protea cynaroides*
ginger see *Zingiber zerumbet*
globe artichoke see *Cynara scolymus*
globe thistle see *Echinops*
gourd see *Cucurbita maxima*
grape hyacinth see *Muscari*
grass
  covering containers 21, 118–19
  decorating containers 80, 115, 158, 180
grasses 40–1, 60–1, 77, 132–3, 177, 215
green pussy willow see *Salix caprea*
guelder rose see *Viburnum opulus*
gypsophila 71

H

hare's tail see *Lagurus ovatus*
hazel see *Corylus avellana* 'Contorta'
headdresses 199
heath sedge see *Carex flacca* 'Schreb'
hellebore see *Helleborus*

hips 18, 96, 152
holly see *Ilex aquifolium*
honeysuckle see *Lonicera periclymenum*
horse-chestnut see *Aesculus hippocastanum*
Hough, Catherine 17

I

Iceland poppy see *Papaver nudicaule*
ikebana 22, 26, 28, 174
ivy see *Hedera helix*

J

Jekyll, Gertrude 22
jonquil see *Narcissus* 'Jumblie'

K

kentia palm 26
king protea see *Protea cynaroides*
kumquat *27, 28*

L

lady's mantle see *Alchemilla mollis*
larch see *Larix*
larkspur see *Consolida*
laurel see *Laurus nobilis*
lavender see *Lavandula*
leaves
  banana 94
  cleaning 176
  covering containers 20, 21, 28, 48–9, 80–1, 132–3
  decorating containers 20, 94, 112–13, 150–1, 162–3
  skeletonized 20
  weaving 150
    see also foliage
leek see *Allium ampeloprasum*
lichen 142–3
lilac see *Syringa*
lily see *Lilium*
lily of the valley see *Convallaria*
lisianthus see *Eustoma russellianum*
lobster claw see *Heliconia*
loosestrife see *Lysimachia*
lotus see *Nelumbo nucifera*
love-in-a-mist see *Nigella damascena*
love-lies-bleeding see *Amaranthus caudatus*
lychee see *Litchi chinensis*

M

Madagascan jasmine see *Stephanotis floribunda*
madonna lily 86
mallow see *Malva*
marigold see *Calendula officinalis*
marjoram see *Origanum*
masterwort see *Astrantia*
milkweed see *Euphorbia*
millet see *Millum*
millet grass see *Pennisetum setaceum*
mimosa see *Acacia*
mind-your-own-business see *Helixine soleirolii*
mock orange see *Philadelphus coronarius*
monkshood see *Aconitum*
montbretia see *Crocosmia*

moss 27, 114, 134, 142, 178, *179*, 222
  see *also* sphagnum moss
mullein see *Verbascum*

N

nature as inspiration 10, 12–21, 130, 136, 166
New Zealand flax see *Phormium tenax*
nosegays 102–5
nutan see *Leucospermum cordifolium*
nuts 134–5, 152, 178

O

oats see *Avena sativa*
old man's beard see *Clematis vitalba* 'Emerald Forest'
onion see *Allium*
orchids 16, 52, 108, 110, 132, 166
oregano see *Origanum vulgare* 'Purple Beauty'
Oudolf, Piet 60

P

painter's palette see *Anthurium andraeanum*
pansy see *Viola wittrockiana*
passionflower see *Passiflora*
pattypan 27
Pearson, Dan 60
pebbles 11, 114
peonies 74 see *also* *Pæonia*
periwinkle see *Vinca major*
Persian buttercup see *Ranunculus*
pin oak see *Quercus ellipsoidalis*
pincushion see *Leucospermum*
pine cones 160, 178
pineapple see *Ananas comosus*
pineapple flower see *Eucomis bicolor*
pink ginger see *Alpinia purpurata*
pitanga see *Eugenia uniflora*
pitcher plant see *Nepenthes maxima*
polyanthus see *Primula*
poppy see *Papaver*
posies 12, 21, 48, 66–7, 92–3
primrose see *Primula vulgaris*
privet see *Ligustrum*
proportion 36, 86, 96, 132
pumpkin see *Cucurbita maxima*

Q

queen palm see *Arecastrum*

R

red-hot pokers see *Kniphofia*
reeds 80, 120, 144, 203
roses 24, 94, 164 see *also* *Rosa*
Royal Gold lily see *Lilium regale*
rue see *Ruta graveolens*
ruscus see *Danäe racemosa*

S

safflower see *Carthamus*
sage see *Salvia*
screw pine reed see *Pandanus odoratissimus*
sea buckthorn see *Hippophäe rhamnoides*
seed heads 40, 77, 88, 112, 146, 156, 199, 203

seeded eucalyptus see *Eucalyptus palanthemos*
silkweed see *Asclepias tuberosa*
silver nitrate solution 100
snake grass see *Equisetum*
snowberry see *Symphoricarpos albus*
snowdrop see *Galanthus Nivalis*
soapwort see *Saponaria*
solidaster 71
South African reed see *Cannomis virgata*
Spanish moss see *Tillandsia usneoides*
sphagnum moss 21, 27, 46, 134, 160, 160
  see *also* *Sphagnum auriculatum*
spring onions 84
Spry, Constance 22
star of Bethlehem see *Ornithogalum thyrsoides*
statice see *Limonium suworowii*
steel grass see *Xanthorrhoea preissii*
stems
  cutting 176
  immersing 45, 76, 88, 100, 114, 176
  rubbing 110
  singeing 76, 176
  strengthening 44, 88, 178, *179*
stock see *Matthiola*
strawberry see *Fragaria*
sunflower see *Helianthus annuus*
Surinam cherry see *Eugenia uniflora*
sweet chestnut see *Castenea sativa*
sweet pea see *Lathyrus odoratus*
sweet violet see *Viola odorata*
sweet william see *Dianthus barbatus*

T

tailflower see *Anthurium andraeanum*
tansy see *Tanacetum vulgare*
techniques
  centrepieces 64–5
  hand-tying
    mixed-flower arrangements 40, 46, 70–1, 92, 122, 126, 177
    single-flower arrangements 62, 130, 158, 177
  informal arrangements 76–9
  large arrangements 42–5
  nosegays 104–5
  presentation 104, 180–1
  table arrangements 80–1
  topiary 16, 18, 21, 27, 34, 58, 90, 98
  treatment of stems 176
  wiring 18, 27, 32, 38, 138, 160, 174, 178–9
throatwort see *Trachelium caeruleum*
tomato see *Lycospericum*
topiary arrangements 26
  bases 90, 98, 174
  cones 27, 98–9
  domes 158–9
  frames 27, 34
  lollipops 16, 34–5, 90–1, 189
  mixed 27, 34–5, 98–9, 189
  single-flower 16, 18, 20, 21, 58–9, 90–1, 140–1
  spheres 58–9, 158 see *also* lollipops above
  techniques 16, 18, 21, 27, 34, 58, 90, 98
Transvaal daisy see *Gerbera*

Turner, Ken 148
twigs 90, 138, 142–3, 144, 160–1, 210

V

vegetables 14, 27, 28, 84–5, 96–9, 178, 191, 197
vines 16, 22, 160
violet see *Viola*
virginia creeper see *Vitis quinquefolia*

W

warratah see *Telopea speciosissima*
water and watering 45, 46, 48, 70, 71, 100, 115
wax flower see *Stephanotis floribunda*
wheat see *Triticum aestivum*
whitebeam see *Sorbus aria* 'Lutescens'
widow iris see *Hermodactylus tuberosa*
wild carrot see *Daucus carota* 'Dara'
wild marjoram see *Origanum vulgare* 'Purple Beauty'
wild oats see *Avena fatua*
wild plantain see *Heliconia*
Williams, Christopher 148, *149*
willow see *Salix matsudana* 'Tortuosa'
Wilson, Dr Ernest 64
wilting 176
witch hazel 16
wood lily see *Trillium*
wreaths 134–5, 160–1, 196

Z

zebra grass see *Miscanthus sinensis* 'Zebrinus'
zinnia 7

Acknowledgments

I have enjoyed immensely working on this book which in some ways is a retrospective of my work over the last fifteen years.

It has been a great pleasure to work again with Kevin Summers and I am most grateful to him for the stunning photography. Kevin adds his own creative eye to my work and I am indebted to him for this input. Thanks also to his charming assistant Vera Kodajova.

A very, very special thanks to Robin Rout and John Crummay who were very instrumental in the look of this book and have been my mentors throughout its development. Thanks also for the 24-hour technical support – you have been my own personal Samaritans!

Thank you to Charles Miers at Rizzoli for the idea and the team at Mitchell Beazley for all their help making it happen. A big thank you to Anna Sanderson who has been very understanding and thanks also to Catherine Emslie, the editor Anne McDowall, and also to Vivienne Brar.

Thanks also to all my staff who have helped with the project and kept the business functioning while I have been distracted by this project. Thanks especially to Sarah Jackson who has juggled helping me with the designs in this book as well as keeping the day-to-day business rolling! Thanks also to the rest of the team who have been so supportive, especially Tania Newman for "everything"!

And also our "freelance" staff Ashleigh Hopkins, Moira Seedhouse, Anita Everard and particularly Samantha Griffiths for all those early mornings and her artistic input on this project!

Thanks to the people who make wonderful vessels in which to arrange flowers: Peter Williams, Vivienne Foley, Catherine Hough, Chris Johnson at Sia, and also the team at LSA.

A huge thank you again to Dennis Edwards for his continued support through the ups and downs of the business and for the help from all my friends at New Covent Garden.

Thanks to our friends who bring the flowers from the fields of Holland, Marcel of MHG flowers and Kees Ross of Ross flowers, Danae Brooks for the stunning Garden roses, Rosebie Morton for her enthusiasm and commitment to growing exciting new varieties, and Ivens Orchids for the best orchids in the world.

And finally thank you to all my friends all over the world that have been collecting my books over the last decade!